Also by Elizabeth Power

Managing Our Selves: Building A Community of Caring
Managing Our Selves: god In Our Midst
How to Get Happier—and why you should try to
Healer: Reducing Crises

Find me at:
httpps:/elizabethpower.com
https:/the-tia.org

If Change Is All There Is

Choice Is All You've Got

by
Elizabeth Power, M.Ed.

Copyright 1992 by Elizabeth Power
Graphics by Karin Griffin

If Chage Is All There Is, Choice Is All You've Got!
Publishing rights@ EPower and Associates, Inc.

All rights reserved. Published by EPower and Associates, Inc.

No part of this publication may be reproduced, or stored in a retrieval system or transmitted in any form by any means electronic, mechanical, photocopying, or otherwise without written permission of publisher. For information about permissions, contact epower@elizabethpower.com, or epower@epowerandassociates.com

ISBN-1-883307-00-7
ISBN 978-1-8843308-004

Printed in the USA

Third edition, November 2025

Introduction

When I was growing up, we used to sit around on Granny's porch and talk.. sometimes we just stood around. One of my favorite photos is of Granny on her porch with her arms crossed, folded up in her apron to keep warm, looking off in the distance. I think there's someone else on the porch with her, but I'm not sure. Doesn't even matter now, because Granny's posture and attitude are what I remember.

We grew up with porch talk. We'd linger there and watch whatever passed by in the back yard in the way of adults or kids in the summer and make talk about what was going on. If there was too big a crowd for Granny's back porch, we'd head for the yard. Didn't matter, it was still porch talk.

Then we'd make talk about whatever we saw going on either on the road (which we could see from that side of the yard) or on the farm next to Granny's and Grampy's place. At night, there would be fires in the outdoor fireplace and the gentle growling of the men's voices.

Sometimes we'd have family reunions at other relatives' places, and we'd all sit on their porch. Some had those great big wrap-around porches and, Lordy, a whole mess of people could talk porch talk there! Size of porch coupled with history of house was a definite indicator of social standing.

I used to believe it was just a rural edge-of-Appalachia Southern phenomenon, but as I talk to folks about it, I find it's spread. I've learned that folks "Not from Here" do it as far away as Michigan and Minnesota. Folks in many places get together and talk about life and its living using their own native dialect and dialogue.

The universal nature of porch talk lies not in the colloquial nature of the phrases and structure or in its community origins. It lies in the nature of parables and metaphor, those ways of communicating the process of living that are less than head on collisions with the truth. It is almost inevitably funny somewhere and most often its humor is not at the expense of someone else.

Porch talk may be slightly catty, gossipy, personal, or even a little tacky; seldom is it blaming or guilt-ridden.

Porch talk talks about all of us somewhere: we've all been so lazy we haven't done enough work to risk breaking the Sabbath sometime, and we've all been nervous as long-tailed cats in rooms full of rocking chairs at some point.

Its beauty is in its ability to relate powerful, perhaps poignant points about living and life. Like living and life, some of its language is awkward, perhaps not quite the epitome of social elegance, and sometimes obscure. Might even need to be read and pondered on for a while.

As a child growing up on porches and in yards, I had no idea of the power of those phrases and stories. As an adult, a person in the business world, finding out how funny they sound to others who grew up in different ways, I see their power. Varying in degree of dialect, depth, and humor, they all relate to getting through life filled with change using the one tool we'll always have: choice.

So, join me. Just pull up a chair, or even symbolically throw your feet up on your desk, and enjoy some porch talk. Sit for a spell, and invite a friend in. Laugh a little, watch night fall, day break, and the shadows shift as the sun courses across the sky. Listen to the sounds of the day where you are, and realize that wherever we are is a porch; whatever we do is where we live our life; and however we live in the changes we face is our story and our legacy to the world that follows us.

Contents

It's a Matter of Conscience 1
That New Spelling 4
Social *What*?? 6
Meeting Mania 8
Exploding Bat Dung 9
Good Grades 11
Takin' Milk Back from Coffee 12
The Vertical Wag 13
Are They Ready? 14
Wait 'til Daylight! 15
Walter's Interview 16
You too? 17
Ambidextrous Pocket Change 18
Budgets 'n Biscuits 19
Bread and Milk 20
Three Companies 21
Hot Dogs or Roast Beef 22
Elevator Story 23
Ambition 24
Southern Astrology: Mama was a Moon Pie 25
Let's Talk about Two Little Threats 26
Grandpa's Black Hat 27
It Takes the Snake Longer to Eat the Hog Than It Does to Kill It! 29
Corn Crop 30
Is the Dirt On Your Neck About To Become the Topsoil On Your Garden? 31
Appearance and Reality 32
Productivity and Poverty 33
Office Politics 35
It's On You Now, Granny! 37
Aunt Eula says, "The Hen's Involved, But The Hog's Committed" 38
Butterflies Don't Like Cocoons 39
I Never Met A Career I Didn't Like 42
Mules, Thunder and Rebellion 44

You Can Stand It 'Til You Die! 46
Self-Discipline Is A Dirty Word 49
Invisible Dogs On Leashes 54
Duck Poots & Whirlwinds 57
Ben Franklin And Failure 62
Information Gluts And Future Shock 67
Iron On Iron 69
Life's Laws Of Physics: Choice Is All There Is 74
Green And Slimy Lazarites 77
Out Of Fear And Into Longing 80
Motivation By Provocation 81
The Myth of Security 83
Rolling Uphill 86
The Rut and the Grave 88
Seasons of Change Paradigms 90
Thermostats and temperaments 94
Feline anxiety 96
Worth Something 98
Gittin older 100
Purty and Pretty 102
A Pointless Job 103
Getting' Close to Finishing 104
The Blight of Terror 105
Not Up to Snuff 106
That dog won't hunt 107
Cheapster | Like a Hair in a Biscuit 109
Grinning like a possum eating saw briars 110
Confused as a termite in a yo-yo 111

It's a Matter of Conscience

If you've even scanned the news, you know there've been a lot of stories about scoundrels and rapscallions in the world lately. It doesn't matter if you're reading about government, business, politics and religion—they've all got their fair share of bad apples in the barrel. It's obvious that there's failings, sadness and badness in people at every level of society.

The high and mighty, politicians and preachers, doctors and daddies, bosses and board rooms, mommies and moguls—every single one shows up with what could be called S-I-N and you don't have to be of any religious persuasion to know what I mean. They get caught doing things that move them away from their definition of "all that is right" or "God" AND away from their own self-identified states of health and wholeness.

In fact, they often get caught in the behavior they rail against at every chance. Shakespeare is credited with saying "Methinks the lady doth protest too much." If you buy in to that statement, whatever someone hollers about the loudest is usually the issue they're dealing with inside of themselves.

I have a friend who says that the three-letter word above is a result of going further, staying longer, and doing more than you mean to. I'm inclined to agree with him.

I bet you could think up at least half a dozen times it's happened and how you or somebody around tried to weasel out of it. I sure can. I think "I'll get this involved and no more" (I don't—I feel good, or the situation makes me feel good, and so I keep right on) or "I'll only stay a couple of hours," or "I'll take this job for right now" (and you know what happens: I get comfortable..or they like me.. and it feels good..and I stay on). And that last one? Oh, I can't *even* begin to tell some of those stories!

It's as if we checking our conscience at the door, if we remembered to bring it in at all! I'd like to "Not me!" and I know I'd be lying. I don't think I've ever checked enough of mine to get away with much. I've certainly made enough amends and learned to listen to it a lot more carefully than ever before since the late '80s.

Truth is, if I'd done as well as I would like to think I have, I wouldn't be writing this tale.

Here a while back, I was in a little rural community named Mulberry. It's not too far a piece from where I grew up, about twenty miles away, and about five hundred feet higher in altitude. In the hills, that's a whole culture—just based on how much higher and how much further back it is. I've got friends there, people that have lived there since the King gave them the land. We were talking about all this badness in the world.

Gary, he's from up there. His people have been there, and even a little higher, for a long time—not as long as his wife, though, whose family has the big house on the land since the 1700s. She began her teaching career when my mother was a teacher. They became fast friends, and I've stayed in touch. They always made a big garden, and I used to help them put up the vegetables. We were stringing beans, and got to talking about this old boy who lives in Hardscuffle, which is *way* back up the holler. He'd been acting the fool and really treating his mother bad. Real bad.

Well, now, Gary, while he was talking, he shook his head while he was telling about how the old boy had took his mama's life savings to buy a bass boat and then got caught stealing a motor for it. On top of that, he beat the boy that caught him stealing it half to death. It looked like he was facing hard time, and from the sound of it, well deserved. Gary said, "I tell you what! He's so rotten, if he had his conscience taken out, it'd be minor surgery!"

I'm thinking there are a lot of people who wouldn't even miss theirs. What happened? How'd it get to be so bad? Is it just more news more often so we hear more about what happens? How is it that **I**, too, get caught up in the fray and toss mine out from time to time?

I wonder have we just left that old conscience behind in search of what we want in the "me-my-mine" world? I don't know. I do know this: if I'm going to live in a world where what I say and do makes life a little easier, and maybe a little better, I **need** my conscience. And it better be so big, and stuck on me so tight that it's just dadgum inoperable. No way to take it out. I want it to grow on me, over me, and in me, until it makes my integrity—because that's what a conscience drives—permanently impeccable.

That New Spelling

One of my uncles, I don't know which one, what side, or how many "greats" attached to his name there were, could have easily told this story about his young nephew. I only heard it sitting around the outdoor fireplace in the soft summertime, or maybe at the cinderblock and wire frame barbeques over at the elementary school yard. The men's civic clubs used to hold them every summer, pressing split chickens between two sets of those woven wire cot bottoms welded to pipe, wired together, and turning them over coals surrounded by cinder block walls. The smoke filled the little courtyard on the back of the little schoolhouse with the wonderful smell of all those seasoned slow cooking chickens.

In the summer, in either place, there'd be older men in soft-worn denim overalls, a little fuzzy around the pockets and round toed work boots or shoes, usually black, with the oil-resistant long wearing heavy soles.

"How's Henry gettin' along in school, Ef?" He said.

"Aw, not so good, Demp. They're learnin' him how to spell 'taters' with a 'P'."

Now for anybody who's got a real commitment to the English language, "taters with a P" just shows how bad somebody's notion of grammar and spelling can be.

But if all you've ever *known* is "taters", tryin' to spell 'em with a "P" is more than a matter of swapping a few letters. Culturally, it **might** even qualify as trying to teach a child how to spell "pig" as "poodle".

It almost assumes there's not a bit of common sense present about the name of a vegetable. I remember the flap about a certain Vice President who couldn't spell potatoes. I know one of the Presidents had trouble with "broccoli." And I suspect more than one wrestled either with a vegetable they couldn't spell or simply didn't like.

In reality, everybody from Idaho to Ireland presented with one would know what it was—regardless of whether they called it a "tater," "patata" potato or "spud"!

Social *What*??

Have you ever noticed that things get shortened the further along we go in life? Now I admit, some things droop and drag, but a lot of things shrink, including my height. The worst thing is we've gotten so dadgum used to acronyms that nowadays people can't even string a whole sentence together! It's all some sort of strange code.

I mean, when I call up about my bank account and get a call center, the first thing I think of when that snippy little thing on the other end asks me for my "social" is *social **what*?!** Social disease? Social status? Social event? In the world I live in, "social " can be followed by a lot of words.

What **they** mean is "Social Security Number." You know, that string of digits assigned at birth that nearly gets tattooed on your rump, and probably would except it'd be too easy to steal for some of us who leave ours exposed as a result of character flaw. And I'll tell you this: when my rump is flapping in the wind, and a truckload of people is about to pass in view, the very last thing I am worried about is that my Social will be seen—there's more at stake than that!

I mean, those people in the call center ought to say what they mean! It's like sayin' "X-mas" instead of "Christmas". If they want my social security number, they ought to ask me for it! All it is is nine little digits.

Call me mean if you want. Every second counts for most of them. They get bonuses when they answer more calls, use less time, make it faster. Not from me. I can be ever so patient asking them "Social what?" I've even been known to say "Ice cream?" and "Single?" and once in a while utter the name of what was once called a social disease to make my point.

    Language is like that. Ask for what you really want: you'll get it. Leave a little room, or try and save a few seconds by uttering some unintelligible ill-defined unclear request, and you may get a very interesting answer.

Meeting Mania

Oh, I *hate* meetings! I don't know many people who don't. Doesn't matter what kind a meetin' or who's holding it. Lemme tell you why.

Number 1: I got a message about where to show up, and *it wasn't*. When they send out an invitation, the least they could do is get the right place on it, or leave a trail to where they've moved to!

Number 2: Somebody sent out a message about what another meetin' was supposed to be about, and whatever they had—I want some! There was no—none whatsoever—resemblance between what they said it was gonna be about and what actually happened. Not a single one of those people coulda followed a path from the henhouse to the outhouse and got their business done!

Number 3: The soap opera meeting format just does not appeal to me. There's the pre-meeting meeting, the meeting, and the post-meeting meeting; and the update to the pre-status status, the status, and the post-status status updates. And . . . the first ten minutes is about the last time, and the next ten minutes is about this time, and then, the last ten minutes is about the next time. And you know what? I don't think those people could get a thing done if they wanted to!

They're like a flock of old Dominicker hens clutching up in the yard outside the coop. They go willy-nilly wild peckin in the dirt until something spooks them, and then they cluster up whinin' and croonin' until one gets too close to the other and all hell breaks loose: it's like an explosion of feathers and racket because one hen got too close to another hen. When they settle down and shake the dust off, not one thing has been accomplished and they sure don't act like it has either.

Number 4: Did not seem in any way they knew who was supposed to do what! It looked like a buncha chickens in a dirt yard, stirrin' up dust and sruttin' their stuff to see who could have the *last* last word. Now I understand peckin' order, and I understand sometimes it does change. But it seemed to me like the dadgum head rooster oughrt to a laid out who was there for what before they got all bollixed up.

Number 5: Talk about talkin'! They were talkin' over each other so much and cell phones and pagers was a-dingin' and a-ringin', it sounded like a collision between a load of tin pans and a crate of ducks! Mmm-mmm.

I still think the best meeting is *not* one! And if there hasta be one, have it standin' up—and when you get done, git gone!

Exploding Bat Dung

Yeah, you know, I'll bet you've never heard this, either:

I was down in Huntsville, Alabama, down at the National Speleological Society (you know, that's them people that goes down in caves with those little hats and lights on and squirms around in the mud and slime and everything).

And this ole boy said to me, "Did you know that lightnin' seeks out bat manure?"

I said, "Naw!"

He said, "Yeah!"

I said, "Naw!"

He said, "Yeah!"

I said, "Naw!"

I said, "Whadda you mean?"

He said, "Well, let me tell you. Lightnin' seeks out bat manure because of the phosphorous in it. ZAPP!! And they explode!"

I said, "Well, I . . . I'll be! I never knowed that!"

Now if you happen to've sought shelter from the storm in a cave—thinking it to be safe—you are in for a real surprise about the time a pile of bat dung blows up in your face! Best as I can figure, it's about like havin' a chicken fly sideways and let loose on you.

You know, you don't have to be too bright to figure out ain't no safer in than out, folks! Fryin's fryin'— be detonated by bat dung in that nice safe cave, or at the risk of lightnin' out in the storm.

Believe I'd rather take the honest risk of the storm.

Good Grades

Well, I'll be, they're talkin' about that little Esther again. Oh, she is so-o –o cute, just a little strawbelle. Tow-headed 'n bright-eyed. She'd rather play than learn. But I never saw such a child that liked to look at bugs and lizards and such as much as Esther.

Still, like her mama says, *school* is Esther's job for the next 12 years. Huh! Esther's not too wild about that. She'd rather be playin' in the creek, catch lightnin' bugs, dig in the dirt, or race June bugs—*anything* but go to school. But . . . she wants to please her mama 'n daddy, so she does try.

This year, her teacher tells me, Esther came in one morning all bright and sunny. Raised her hand first thing in class, 'cause she had somethin' for the "Tell" part of "Show and Tell". Looked like a little worm in hot ashes wigglin' in her seat, with that hand straight up in the air.

"Yes, Esther, what is it?" teacher asked.

"I don't want to scare you," Esther piped up. "But my papa said if I didn't get better grades, somebody's gonna get a whoopin' . . .!!

Takin' Milk Back from Coffee

Resa told it to me, she sure did! We was a-sittin' on the porch lookin' down yonder, and she said that Loy had come home upset. His boss had read him the riot act over somethin' he didn't no way do!

Well, I tell you what, we sat there a little while, and watched that earthmover just dig that ole red clay around down on the MacMillan place. And Loy come back, and he was grinnin' like a cat eatin' tuna. He said his boss had apologized!

She said, "Some people—just like Loy's boss—I reckon they think you can take milk back from coffee. Once you done poured it in, it's *in*!"

The Vertical Wag

"Oh, today's office su-u-rely is different," Upie said. "Why, when I was plant manager, I had a *real* office! Not these little cracker-box things with no doors and no walls to the ceilin'. I thought they was a-callin' 'em 'cuticles' 'til my wife tole me better.
Ethel, *she* says they're called 'cubicles'.

But what I *really* wonder is if anybody's got any dadgum room! The last time I was up to where the wife works, that cubicle was so small, even a *little* dog woulda had to wag his tail up and down instead of sideways!"

Are They Ready?

Jim Bob, he walked up to the fella in the white coat by the dairy case. Looked him up and down, cast that eyeball on him lo-on-ng and hard. Then Jim Bob nodded his head back towards the dairy case where all those eggs were neatly stacked up in cartons, sorted by grade and color.

"Those eggs fresh?" he asked.

Mr. White-Coat, Hair-All-Slicked-Back, looked Jim Bob up and down, figurin' him to be a customer right on the edge of bein' cranky. And honey, he didn't know the half of it! Jim Bob looked like the type to complain about every little thing. Why, he'da complained if you hung him with a new rope!

"Randy!" that dairy case manager hollered out.

"Yessir!"

"Feel those eggs. Check and see if they're cool enough to sell!"

Wait 'til Daylight!

I tell you what, that Sam was determined to throw up a barn fer his new tractor. Wouldn't *nothin'* do 'til he could get his lumber in and get a few fellers together to frame it up with him.

Now Sam, he was an impatient feller. When he wanted it done, he wanted it done! Right now, and I mean, *R-A-T-N-O-W* now!

Well, the appointed date came, and Sam, he was chompin' at the bit at daylight. He was *so* ready, it was like he had new, fresh batteries put in. But the boys apparently got a better offer.

He waited until he was pretty certain they wasn't gonna show up, and he lit into it. He snorted and he stomped, and he heaved and he hoed. He worked around, he'd frame it hisself, by golly, and that's all there was to it!

It passed lunchtime and it passed dinnertime, and he hadn't come into the house at all. Just a hammerin', hammerin', hammerin'. And when the fireflies was high in the oak trees, he come in out of the yard.

Now his daddy had been a-watchin' him since before dusk. Just a-sittin' in an old al-u-min-i-um foldin' chair. He looked at Sam as he got near. Looked him up and down, and cast that long eyeball on him, and shook his head and said, "Sam! It takes a he-e-eap a licks to strike a nail in the dark!"

Walter's Interview

I'll be squat. You know, Walter, he was interviewin' for an executive position. Hit's not that we ever felt he could be an executive, now mind you, just that we were glad he was gettin' the interview.

So the day of the interview come.

"Why do you feel you can do this job?" the personnel woman asked Walter. She looked down over her glasses while she twirled her pencil.

Walter, he scrotched his head and looked right thoughtful for a minute. "Well," he said, "Things change so fast, I figger I couldn't be wrong *all* the time!"

See, we didn't expect Walter to get no executive position, because when his time came to drink from the Fountain of Knowledge, we're pretty certain he only gargled. And if it's true that what a body don't know won't hurt 'em, why Walter, he's a lucky dog; he'd be damn right invulnerable. His mama said, "It's kinda like the wheel's still turnin', but the hamster's dead!"

You too?

    Let me tell you what, now! I never knew anybody—I mean *anybody*—to change, jest 'cause you whooped 'em.

    Lizzy, Maggie, Tody 'n Poley, they all knew not to run from a whippin'. Only meant it was worse when they got it. So one day, poor little Tody was just wore out with his mama, and he didn't deserve a whippin' and he wasn't gonna take one! So he off and laid up underneath the foundation of the house, workin' his way further and further back in that red dirt crawl space.

    Now his Mama knew where he was at, and every time she went over that wooden floor where he was, she'd stomp re-e-al hard to let him know that she knew he was there. Lizzy, Maggie and Poley had done took their whippin's, and they could hardly wait to see what Mama was gonna do to Tody. (Or better yet, what Daddy would do, whenever he got home).

    Daddy come home. Miz Ruby—now that was Tody's mama—she told him about Tody. So he went and crawled up under the house, sayin', "Tody! Tody, you under here?"

    And pretty soon he was over near where Tody was. And Tody said, "Daddy, is she after you, too?!"

Ambidextrous Pocket Change

"What's that new hire like, Sadie?" Rosie had her old clipboard propped up on her hip. Oo-ooh, she was a looker! Luscious like.

She'd been a supervisor for the longest time, why started as soon as she was old enough. That Rosie, she knew that plant inside and out. Call *her* a "linthead", and she'd take it as a compliment!

Sadie, on the other hand, done got herself a new toe sewer on the third shift. Rosie swapped stories about her new jularker and a hot date at the drive-in theater for Sadie's sad tales of farm life. Sadie, bright enough, was right plain lookin..

"Mercy, Rosie, it's like she's left-handed, and keeps her change in her right hand pocket. Has trouble with the simplest instructions. Don't hardly know left from right. I am not sure she's gonna make it." Sadie shook her head. "When I saw her about to use a metal screwdriver on a 'lectric war? It was like she's livin' in a 100-watt world with a 40-watt bulb!"

Rose said, "She better figger out which pocket's which!"

Budgets 'n Biscuits

I was sittin' down talkin' to some buddies of mine the other day back up in Mulberry. I spend a lot of time just watchin' things go by. And I've got a friend up there. And she asked me, "Whadda you reckon a "budget" is?

I said, "I'll tell you what's the gospel truth. All I can figure is, it's a thing to git you to worry beforehand instead of afterwards!"

And she said back to me, "No, let's put it in a bigger context. Let's put it in context of a recession. "

I said, "I believe that a recession is a time when you've gotta tighten the belt. But now, a depression is when they ain't got no belt to tighten"

She said, "Yeah?"

I said, "'N I believe that we're pretty close to a panic, because a panic is when they's not no pants to hold up nor a belt to tighten 'em with!"

Y' know what she said back to me? She said, "If you think it's a problem now, you just wait 'til the government solves it!"

I said, "Sister, long as I got a biscuit, you've got half!"

Bread and Milk

This ole boy come in the drugstore and sat down at the soda counter. Now I suspect there are a lot of you who don't remember such things as a soda counter. For those of you who don't—you could walk in a drugstore or the Five 'N Dime or the Woolworth's or whatever variety store there was that had a little lunch counter, and you'd see all kinds of business people. It'd prob'ly be the equivalent of our golf course these days.

So this ole boy, he come in and plopped down on a stool and sat himself there and ordered bread and milk. And the feller on the stool next to him looked over, kinda squinched his eyes up, and said, "Y'on a diet?"

Ole boy said, "Nope! On a commission!"

Three Companies

Sally, she was in with her boss, talkin' about she wanted a raise. In fact, she said, "*I deserve* a raise!"

He said, "Hunh—Why on earth do you think you deserve a raise?"

And Sally, she brought her chin up a little higher in the air, and she looked down her little nose at him and said, "Why, there are three companies after me!"

"Really?!" her boss said. "Which ones?"

"Light, gas and water!" she said.

Hot Dogs or Roast Beef

I tell you what, I was up at the house th'other day, and my cousin, he come up and he said to me, "Listen, we're havin' dinner down here at the big house. You wanna come down here and join us?"

I said, "Why, that'd be great!"

He said, "Well, what do you want? Do you want hot dogs or roast beef?"

I said, "Oh, I hadn't had good roast beef in a long time."

He said, "Yeah, we're havin' hot dogs!"

And you know what, that's about what life is like. You think you've been offered a choice, and you don't have one at all!

Elevator Story

Two friends of mine and their passel of little young'uns live so far back up in the hills, you'd just about have to swing a kudzu vine to get across to their house. No TV! And—worse yet—no electricity. Lived "off the grid", as they say! Which of course, clearly meant they were livin' in the Dark Ages.

Eumia, she decided it was time to carry little Ruby to town, so she could learn about modern ways in the world she would soon face if she left home. So they got a neighbor lady who lived close by, a friend, to carry 'em down to the shoppin' center

They were particularly fascinated by these steel plates with a seam down the middle that seemed to open and close just as if by magic. They stood there and they watched and they watched while this old feller—Lord, he looked like Methuselah, looked like he'd been rode hard and put up wet—got in there, and the plate slid shut. And they stood there just a watchin' and a-watchin'.

And here in a few minutes, the plates opened up, and out come this young good-lookin' man.

And Eumia, what she did. I'll be if she didn't say, "Come on, young'un, let's go get Paw!"

Ambition

These little ditties came to me by way of a number of people over the years, and they're about the best thing you could say about ambition:

"It's real simple. You cain't fall out of bed if you sleep on the floor!" Now, y'all don't have to be brain surgeons to figure that one out. While it certainly reduces the risk of falling, it can shorely make for a backache in the morning.

Now, this one's more modern: "Give a man a fish, and you feed him for a day. Teach him to use the Internet, and he won't bother you for weeks! And if you want him gone for a year? Get him connected with AI."

Then there's "You can't reap what you don't sow." That's kind of like we all want to be millionaires, we just don't want to get there. If you don't plant the seeds of success in your garden of life, it's unlikely you'll have it.

Lucy said, "She aint gonna hoe a long row." And she was right, Althea was, well, just lazy. Never did a moment's more work than she could avoid. We could never tell if it was ambition or ability. She never took a step, said a word, or did a thing more than necessary.

It's all about ambition: what you want to put in your pocket, what you want to leave behind when you shuffle off this mortal coil, and what you want to put in your heart.

Some folks look to a tall ladder in heart, hand, or wallet. Some are happy just to sit on the bottom step.

Southern Astrology: Mama was a Moon Pie

You know, according to the signs, my mama woulda been a "moon pie". I think she was mis-assigned at birth. Moon pies are the type that spends a lot of time on the front porch. Not her.

It's a cinch to recognize the physical appearance of moon pies. *Big* and *round* are the key words here. (Not my mama, she had a lifetime chip from Weight Watchers and the figure to match).

You should marry anybody who you can get remotely interested in the idea. It's not gonna be easy! Well, Bert approached her, 20 years after Daddy died and without more than a handful of dates.

There was that time Granny was having pulpwood cut and Mr. Whatshisname showed up at the front door in long johns, overalls, and a hat with a chiceken in one hand and a shotgun in the other. I"ma lookin fer a wife," he said. "No thank you," she erplied and shut the door. We were a little worried about the house getting burned down for a while. I don't know if that counts.

This might be the year to think about aerobics! Nah. She's been ashes since 1989. Uh-uh—maybe not!

Let's Talk about Two Little Threats

Threats have a bi-i-g place to play in dealin' with change and makin' life better! Sometimes you just got to lay one down to help somebody out.

And the first one that got laid on me this week was: "This'll jar yer preserves!" And I'm tellin' you what, she did indeed jar my preserves—right out of the can!

And you know what I said back to her? I said, "Honey, I'll slap you so hard, your clothes'll be outta style!"

So I eyeballed her with the big old stink eye, and silently put the hoodoo on her. She warnt getting a piece of my life, and I wouldn't cut my hair within a mile of her. One of my girlfriends who was there? She cocked her head up and said "It looks to me like you run her out the back door—and that is definitely the place she ort to be."

She swiveled around to me and said, "An' let that be a lesson for you, miss gypsy-foot. Don't make us have to give ye a bedsheet beatin' to settle ye down."

Grandpa's Black Hat

I have an uncle who went up in the hills. Sell a little in-surance now 'n then. And he went up to see if he could write a few policies, and it come up a freshet. Now, when you say "It come up a freshet," what that means is, it started rainin' re-e-al hard!

And my uncle, he went down the mountain, went down a little road to the bridge down at here, and it was washed out. So he thought he'd climb back up across the ridge and go to the bridge at yonder and see if it was still OK to cross. But he got there, and—wouldn't you know it? —the bridge at yonder, it was done under water, too!

So he clumb back up the ridge and got out and dashed through the rain up to the porch and said, "Now Mrs. Cannon, do you mind if I set a spell?"

She said, "Lo-o-rd, no, boy. But pull y'up a chair."

So he pulled up a chair, and he was sittin' on the porch with her, and they could hear the rain on the tin roof and the lightnin' crackin' down in the valley and the thunder rolliin' back through the hills. They were just kinda sittin' there, not sayin' a whole lot.

And here in a little bit, my uncle, he looked up here and he said, "Mrs. Cannon, can you he'p me out?"

She said, "Whadda you mean, boy?"

He said, "Well," he said, "Now I know I been called *queer*—and I even been called *tetched*. He said, "But I can't fer the life of me figure out what I'm a-lookin' at!"

She said, "Whadda you mean?"

He said, "Well, down yonder, I know good and well that creek runs west ta east. But I'm seein' a black hat go north 50 yards and then south 50 yards, and north 50 yards and south 50 yards, and north 50 yards and south 50 yards.

She said, "Aw, law, boy, don't pay that no nevermind! That's just Grandpa. He said come heck er high water, he's goin' mow that yard today!"

It Takes the Snake Longer to Eat the Hog Than It Does to Kill It!

I'll be! I'm tellin' you what, now! How long does it take a tornado to strike—especially if there's a mobile home park near-by?! Or for somebody to bet on your business and throw it in a tizzy, or to say the words *I - want - out!!!*?

It doesn't take a whole lot of time! It takes a who-ole lot less time than it does to clean up, calm people down, and work out all the details.

Snake'll sit, it'll watch, and watch, and watch. And then it'll strike! Let's say it strikes a hog. Now that's not likely, but it could happen. Snakes are as scared of hogs as people are of change. Hogs, it's said—and I don't know if I believe it or not—are immune to snake venom. S

Jest like it'd take a snake a lon-ng time to stuff a hog down its double-hinged jaw, it's gonna take a lon-ng time to adjust to change.

So you got a computer modem that ties you in and lets you know a day ahead of time your business is bein' sold? So you're a professional tornado spotter, and you know it's gonna hit your place? Or maybe it takes somebody six months to say, "I want out!"

No matter how long it takes for the change to happen, it still takes longer to adjust to change than it does to create it!

Corn Crop

Crop failure—it's a common thing where I come from.

Smith, he was sittin' at the table with Greg, comparin' just how bad the crop failure in his history had been.

"Ay-yeah, they's been some bad droughts in my time! Why back in Nineteen and Ninety-Six, the corn crop was so scramped, that when we fried up some for dinner, we ate a dozen acres in one meal!" Smith rared back in his split oak chair and hooked his thumbs under his galluses.

Greg said, "Yeah, I know. Remember that summer was so dry the trees was paying the dogs to pee on 'em?" He shook his head.

Smith nodded. "Ay-uh."

"But last year? Whoo Lordy it made up for a few. Just the right amount of sun, heat and water topped with a heaping dose of fertilize. Every stalk had at least six ears on it. I swan I thought we'd for sure hired the bees." Greg retorted.

Smith nodded. "Ay-uh. Sure was a juicy crop, just like that old Doublemint® gum this wuz like gittin two for the price of one."

Greg grunted. "Horse corn didn't do good though. Too much water for it."

Smith grunted. "Ay-uh."

Is the Dirt On Your Neck About To Become the Topsoil On Your Garden?

    Listen! This whole thing isn't anything but a garden story! You start out, and you look at the weeds, and you dig 'em up. Change comes along, and you plant some seeds. You weed some weeds. You till some dirt.

    Now if the dirt on your neck is about to become the topsoil on your garden, the first thing is, you could think you're so poor you can't afford to give it away. You might as well just let it get to be ruddy wrinkles. Let the sun weather it. Let it turn red, make your white socks orange. Keep it.

    But you know what? Come spring, you're gonna have to deal with that garden again! You can slough the dirt off your neck and use it as the topsoil on your garden. That's some rich dirt—dirt that's had your life tilled in it. It'll feed that ground and enrich it. Make things grow better. Give you more confidence. Help you have both hams on your hips at market, unlike the poor hog who loses their hams in the meat barn.

You can become supple steel, have no grave cloths and rattle the chains of change with the power of deliberate choice.

Appearance and Reality

There are three things my mama used to say to me.

The first one was, "The price of yer hat is not the measure of yer brain." I totally get it. I'm still me whether I'd dressed rich or poor, fancy or plain. My brain—my mind, what I know, how I think—are so much more than any external look could ever be.

She got this next one from my great-grandpa, who was a horse trader. She said that he said, "Cuttin' off a mule's ear don't make it a horse!" Mm-hmm. True that. I cannot tell you how many times I've heard myself say "Don't pee on my leg and tell me it's raining." It's the same kind of thing.

And then, I think she probably got this one from somebody else: "If you can't see the bottom, don't wade!"

These are all about seeing things the way they are and responding appropriately: people may have more money than sense, beware of someone trying to you tell you something isn't what it, and you might want to think about to secure your safety.

Productivity and Poverty

My grandpa from Georgia had a mouse in the house. He'd be asleep in the bed and hear it scurrying around. Then he'd hear the mouse jump down on the grain bucket and help itself. It had gotten right chubby. He couldn't get it to eat what was in the mousetrap, the cat didn't care, and the old man was just generally cranky about it. He didn't like that mouse at all and wished it all kinds of wickedness.

He sat up one night with his pistol in his hand, ready to shoot that mouse off the grain bucket. He sat real quiet in the chair by the door, just across from the grain bucket. He'd moved anything he might break if he shot at the mouse, trying to appease my Grandmother.

He waited that one night, and the mouse didn't come. Two nights went by. On the third night, there was a big full moon comin in through the window, and he just waited. The mouse finally showed up, scurrying right easy like, stopping to sniff every step or so. It climbed up the wood pile and jumped across to the bucket.

Grandpa took aim. Pulled the trigger. Boom!!! He got the mouse and the grain bucket at the same time. He set his gun down in his lap, and waited. He knew what was next.

When she heard the shot, Grandmother shrieked. She jumped up and came boiling of the bed room, her mob cap (she wore it to keep her hair neat) all out of whack, lookin wild eyed and gave him the dickens for shootin' in the house. "Like to skeert me to death!" she said, wagging her finger. She wore him out for shooting the gun, soiling the grain with mouse guts, and making a hole in the bucket. Then she went "Hmph!" and squared up her shoulders, arms a kimbo. All the while, the grain was trickling out the hole in bucket.

Grandpa just looked up at her, and he cocked one eyebrow, and he said, "Minnie, it's a poor mouse that sits on a sack and doesn't gnaw!"

Office Politics

Oh, man, don't you just hate 'em?! I'm tellin' you what, now. There's nothin' worse than tryin' to live through office politics. Mmh!

You know, you look at some of these fellas, and they go around and they talk outta both sides of their mouth. You know what we say about that up home? "He's like a hog that's left its tracks on both sides of the creek!"

You know, one of the things I learned early on is, there's two sides to everything. Admittedly, yorta hear both of them before making up your mind. That is, if it's any of your business to begin with. And often it's not. It's Otis mad at Rance who's telling Oofie all about it and Oofie doesn't have any part of it.

The hardest thing in the world is to tell people to shut up. Be quiet. Not tell tales, not try to get you on their side. To let it sit. I guarantee you, if Oofie tells Rance he don't want to hear about it, Rance is gonna get mad.

It's kind of like trying to explain to a five year old that there really are two sides to fly paper and it makes a lot of difference to the fly which one he chooses! The little kid doesn't quite "get" the "two sides" thing and you don't want to let them stick their hand to the fly paper on both sides. Of course, that might be the fastest way to help them learn, and the messiest. They almost can't keep their hands still.

Of all the things Oofie doesn't get, bless his heart, we're pretty sure God didn't give with both hands when He was giving Oofie smarts, that's the big one. What is his business, what's not, and how to stay of everybody else's.

We're real proud he might tell Rance that he needs to take that up with Otis, since it's between him and Otis, and we're real sad that Rance will huff off and be mad at Oofie over it. Probably go spread it to everbody except Otis, and maybe him too.

Rance is just shuffling blame around like it's a hot potato. He don't know that if he just lets it sit it'll cool right off. So will Otis, or at least be more reasonable to talk to.

It's On You Now, Granny!

Now, when I was a young-'un, my granny was my absolute most favorite person in the world. Why, she could make banana puddin' like nobody else could. She could soothe my sores like nobody else could. And she was a fine musician. She collected more stuff than Carters has got little liver pills!

And Granny used to watch me play like nobody's business. I'd be out diggin' little bugs, and breakin' tails offa lizards, and racin' June bugs, and all kinds of things.

I didn't mind playin' with 'em. But I sure, Bud, didn't want 'em on me!

Well I'll be, if one day I didn't get one on me! And I went runnin' to Granny, first thing off. And she was lookin' and a-searchin' and a-pokin' and tryin' to find that bug! And I was squirmin' and carryin' on like nothin' you've ever seen.

And all of a sudden, I got real still. And here in a second, she sat back, and she looked up, and she said, "I cain't find it! Where is it?"

I looked up at her with these big old Chinquapin eyes, and I said, "It's all right! It's on you now, Granny!"

And everything was OK.

Aunt Eula says, "The Hen's Involved, But The Hog's Committed"

I am always just gobsmacked how much people would rather suffer than change. Does that ever strike you funny? You see people who stay in awful situations, refuse to do anything different, hunkered down like skeert rabbits. Let me go a little further with the animals here.

Forget the rabbit. It's more kind of like a country breakfast: the hen's involved, but the hog's committed. Only thing the hen does is lay an egg. Old hog gives up his bacon. He only gets one go at it. You don't see many hog-amputees on platforms with four wheels and a couple of plumber's aids scooting around the hogpen.

Too many times, we act like we're hogs. Act like asking or requiring us to change is like asking us to give up a haunch to get a concert ticket. Seems like we need to tweak that around. Truth is, we're a lot more like hens. Every time we go through change, we lay an egg.

Now, each time that hen sets, she comes up off the nest different. Never the same after each egg. Same with us. We sure squawk enough! Everybody in the area usually knows we're different by the time it's done. Her? She's hollerin to tell the rooster to come lead her back to where all the other hens are scratchin.

Makes more sense to set and lay than to give up a side of bacon!

Butterflies Don't Like Cocoons

  I was all wropped up in the bed on the first cold night and thrashing around trying to unwind the covers. All of a sudden, I thought about what might be like to be a caterpillar on the way to becoming a butterfly. Imagine finding yourself driven to start spinning your own closet! If caterpillars have any sense of self at all, I think it would be quite a shock. Who could relish the thought of being wrapped up, unable to move and not knowing what's next? When or whether you might emerge? Hard position to be in, unless you're some kind of perpetual optimist or pre-informed—and caterpillars have pretty slim chances to be either.

  It was shock enough to try to find my way out of a couple of quilts and a comforter in which I had hopelessly entangled myself in my sleep. I'd gotten so bolluxed up I had to wake up fully, look at all the tangles and then slowly and deliberately unwind and unloose them. I think if I'd work up from a bad dream in that state I mighta thought I was being held hostage or tied up. Coulda gone frantic easily.

  I'm surprised caterpillars don't go frantic as they change. Without knowing what is happening, their body changes, they experience the urge to gnaw through he shell, work with a sense of urgency beyond belief to break out.

  Little Emma recently found a cocoon in the process of hatching. She thought the butterfly was in trouble, so she decided to give Mother Nature a hand. She gently tore away the carefully spun encasing, let the butterfly emerge with its folded and rumpled wings, set it on her finger, and then blew on its wings.

The butterfly hadn't exerted a dab of effort breaking out of its cocoon. It couldn't fly. In fact, it died. What Little Emma didn't realize was that the butterfly had to struggle in order to strengthen its wings and to force bodily fluids through its veins to finish developing to fullness.

Many times in the depths of personal or professional change, that old cocoon is real appealing. It may be the cocoon of "Them Versus Us" or "They're Out To Get Me." It may be the cocoon of "We've Always Done It That Way." If I hadn't of needed to get up, I might scrunched back down under the tangled covers.

Caterpillars become butterflies only by making cocoons, thrashing and struggling for the right length of time as they come out, and then by beating their wings in the air before taking off. Not spinning the cocoon, trying to come out early or late, or well-intentioned wrong kinds of help kills them. They have to do it on their own.

It's the process that makes them beautiful.

When a business is opened, sold, or closed, it requires the people in it to shed their old cocoons. So does divorce, being widowed, getting married. Most major changes do—they call out a sort of transparency necessary to make the transition. It would be easier to stay just the same, keep on being the old caterpillar.

It's easier. Shedding the cocoon, risking doing something different is scary. I understand that; it's just plain difficult. Feels like taking a psychotic break instead of a lunch break. Kind of like coming with a full load of bricks mentally and choosing to get "one brick short of a full load" for a while.

But: look at the outcome.

I Never Met A Career I Didn't Like

That lady recruiter looked at me, her glasses down on her nose. She was barely old enough to have younguns. Had a big old twirly updo with a chopstick stuck in it.

"You've certainly had a lot of jobs in different areas," she said, one eyebrow crawling off her forehead. "Are you what we'd call a job hopper?"

For a while, I looked at all the changes as instability and indecisiveness. Finally I recontexted it. I considered it another way: Each time I added more to my knowledge base, learned more, put more into my brain that helps me do what I do now. I'm a whole lot more of who I can become because I've done a lot of different types of work.

"No, ma'am," I replied carefully. "I'd say I'm someone who can do a lot of things very well who has helped a lot of folks get where they want to go.

"For example, when I was a shoe repairer, I learned a lot about how people feel about something as simple as their shoes. I learned the measure of a person isn't in their wallet, but in how they treat service employees. My clients included country music stars like Tammy Wynette, Minnie Pearl, and Alabama. The ones who treated me like a valuable asset in their lives helped me see my skill as a gift, and that I was important to them."

"When I worked in the state's human services function and got threatened with a write-up for being over-productive in adoption and foster home recruitment for special needs kids? I learned about how being too far above average was as bad as being too far below it. I learned that systems, even public ones, needed people in trouble to be able tro have clients to generate revenue. So I quit to become an entrepreneur.

"When I struggled for fifteen years to make an idea come trie about how we respond to tough times? And still kept going until there warnt no go left? I learned we're all attached to our misery and to old ways of thinking that keep us colonized like ants in an ant farm. I learned massive action tools, how to identify and adjust processes on the fly, how timing was the most important thing in many aspects of business.

"In fact, I'd say I learned more in these three fields that I did anywhere else in my life. All three were the school of hard knocks." I held my head high. "I've never met a career I didn't like, even when I failed at it. They've all been good teachers."

Mules, Thunder and Rebellion

A mule won't move if he don't want to. Go against his wants, and he just puts it in park. Period. About the only way you can get one to go then is pry up his tail and put a burr under it—if you're big enough to do it! And if it's thunderin? No way. Only takes about once of gettin' your head clobbered by a mule kick to learn just how independent and merely tolerant of people mules are. Mule trainers aren't called muleskinners for nothin'!

Mules work hard. They work steady. And they despise change.

Just like a mule, lot of folks just sit still when they hear thunder comin' up the valley, too. They might be on the porch sittin' in their rockers, hear that rumblin' rollin' up the valley and just keep on sittin' even though anybody with any sense knows it means a storm is comin'.

If you combine the stubbornness of a mule with a tendency we all have to just stay put when we hear thunder rumblin', you got trouble!

Remember when you were a kid? You probably had a "crick," drainage ditch, or some other body of water nearby. And in the middle of winter, your mama said to you "Don't you dare get in that water! You'll absolutely catch your death of a cold if you do. I'll wear you out if you so much as set one toe in that crick! You hear me?"

Or sometimes Mama said, "Don't look at me in that tone of voice", and I knew exactly what she meant. Trouble is, threats like that just made me act like the old mule. I went into rebellion so fast it made Mama's head swim. Put it in Park and stayed there.

You think about it: Didn't you get in the crick, read under the covers, wait 'til the last minute or cross the invisible line?

Want to see a bunch of mule-like people sitting down out of stubbornness?
Get paralyzed with fear (we do that a whole lot more often!)? Freeze at the sound of thunder in the valley? Maybe even get so stove up that a burr under their tail won't even move them?

Just do them the way you got done that made you rear up and rebel.

You Can Stand It 'Til You Die!

Faema held her head in her hands. "I just can't stand it, I can't take any more—I'll die if anything else happens!" I've heard lots of people say that in the middle of corporate transitions, takeovers, and divestitures—not to mention people in the middle of painful personal situations like death, divorce, disease or dismissal from work. She'd just buried her father, then her work laid her off and on top of that, she'd just learned she needed surgery.

I once heard Albert Ellis speak. He was sitting on a chair, legs crossed, on stage, with a tiny table next to him. Smoking like a steam engine. He takes a long deep draw on this cigarette, blows smoke into the air upwards, and growls, "There's a guy being run over by a steam roller. He's screaming 'I can't stand it! I can't stand it! Oh my God, I can't stand it!' You can stand it until you die. He will. I will. You will." With that, he took another drag of his smoke and exhaled straight in front of him.

Pain is part of change and growth (remember the butterfly?) just like awkwardness, irritation, embarrassment, fear and anxiety are. Often we feel really stupid, wonder maybe even what's the point? How can we stand it?

Of course you can survive it. And you'll stand it until you die. The question is, using what coping mechanisms?

A certain amount of American toughness in how we stand events that are painful went out when we began to be a self-focused and fairly narcissistic society. When did "we" and "us" become "I" and "me"? It feels like it began a little before the COVID pandemic, and has just kept up. With that shift went a certain resilience, a certain cohesiveness that made it possible for us to mourn our losses as a nation and as significant groups. Like work groups.

I am not necessarily an advocate of grief groups at work, now mind you. I am an advocate of reality based thinking. No one ever promised any of us jobs until death do us part. No one ever guaranteed us we'd have it made regardless of how competent (or incompetent?) we were. Fairness is also not promised. Neither is loyalty. There are no guarantees in life.

Instead of bemoaning the loss of perceived guarantees to life, liberty, and happiness the way we want it, striving to find meaning in our experiences of change is a far more powerful idea.

Instead of becoming martyrs, masochists or madmen why not become people of strength who can face the unknown with courage and grace, and go on?

Whatever happened to grit, pluck, and persistence? So what if it didn't go the way you wanted it to—what might this path bring? So what if you hurt—embrace it and heal instead of wallowing. So what if you lost a job you really liked: chances are you don't own all the choices. So what if it's uncomfortable: maybe it's time to slow down and see where the rub is.

You can stand it 'til you die—like Albert Ellis said. The sooner you realize it, hurt (normal), holler, and go on, the sooner you get on with the richness of life that's waitin' for you. Yes, you might cry like a rat eatin' onions, and you need to keep going. Even if it's half an inch at a time.

Part of life is the challenge of how to go through the challenging times, and many of us have learned to shrink instead of stand. Knowing how to do both makes it much easier.

Self-Discipline Is A Dirty Word

You bet it is. Every time I've tried to use self-discipline as I originally learned it, I've really bolluxed things up. Bad. It just gives me a hard way to go. Does it you?

Think about it: Every area where you use self-discipline. Dieting. Saving money. Rearing kids. Working with other people.

Now, we all know some people who have a lot of inner strength who deal with these areas differently. They don't go around self-flagellating and beating themselves to a pulp every time they try something. They set up success instead of failure, and do it by dint of will and belief in the outcome.

As for me, and lots of other people, it's a whole different process.

Most of us get taught self-discipline the same way. Along about the time we begin to learn language and walk, we toddle into the kitchen and reach for a red hot stove eye. We say, "'Tove, Mommy?" and hear the reply, "Yes, baby, that's a stove, No—don't touch it. You might get burned." That reply soon becomes a litany, repeated over and over again as we work into learning personal safety, and about the parts of our world.

One day, though, we toddle into the kitchen, reach for the hot burner, and ask again, "'Tove, Mommy?" and this time get a very different response. "If I've told you once, I've told you fifteen thousand times, stay away from the stove!" It carries the unusual emphasis of a hand on the rear as well, more often than not, and is the ultimate expression of how we are taught self-discipline at an early age.

Most of us slink off crying and feeling ashamed of ourselves at that point, and are darn sure we won't ask again.

School is not without its perils, too, in the area of self-discipline. Since children spend the majority of their day there, more than their waking hours at home, it becomes the place where most social behavior is modeled.

The education system helped you to learn about socially acceptable behavior in groups, how to handle yourself in a learning environment, how to delay gratification by completing required work before you played, how to be obedient. All of that required self-discipline.

How did it help you learn self-discipline? Well, start with restriction. Did you ever get kept back from an activity? Or restricted to a study hall? If not, maybe it was monitoring that got you trained—you know, dealing with Teach who had eyes in the back of her head and could see everything you were doing. No?? How about restraint? You might have had to stand in a corner, sit in the closet, put your nose in a circle, go to time out. If all else failed, you were punished. "I will not throw spitwads" 1000 times pretty well took your spitwad title away, didn't it? Remember trying to use three pencils at once? I can guarantee that anyone dieting or trying to achieve a desired goal who uses self-discipline probably uses one or more of the above techniques to motivate themselves.

No one likes feeling deprived of something they want, even if it's to get something else they want. Most of us use negative, punitive premises at some time in the process of self-discipline. The way we learn self-discipline, we beat ourselves to a bloody pulp trying to get to something that we really want. It doesn't make much sense if you think about it. Using a "No" process to get to a "Yes" goal is pretty skewed thinking.

Did you know that the root word for disciple and discipline are the same? The Latin "discipulus," meaning to follow, is their root.

Every process of discipleship has four common steps. Whether you look at a spiritual or secular figure, from Jesus Christ to Hitler, the steps are the same. The four conscious steps are:

1. Encountering the teacher to whom one becomes a disciple.

2. Choosing consciously to follow that teacher.

3. Changing progressively over time to more and more closely follow the teacher's teachings.

4. Being taught through acceptance.

A classic example in the spiritual is Peter, the itinerant fisherman who chose to follow Jesus. Hopefully, he knew how he got there the morning after he said "Yes" and began to follow Jesus. He didn't become the spiritual leader he ended up overnight—he struggled with his identity, with the problem of being associated with "them" after Jesus' trial. Further, in the garden of Gethsemane where the soldiers came to arrest Him, he drew a sword and cut off Malchus' ear. Hardly in keeping, I'd say, with his teaching. Did Jesus kick him out of the group? Restrict him? Restrain him? Tell him he'd better watch out from here on out? Punish him? Hardly. He reminded Peter of who He was and of the necessity of the events they were experiencing. After he'd put Malchus' ear back where it came from.

Now, I hate to use this example, and the same is true for Hitler. The people who chose, even as opposed to choosing death, to follow Hitler and become Nazis learned the precepts and behavior of Nazism over time. Had Hitler simply had every person killed who fell short of the program, he never would have had people in command and the organization he had. Couldn't have happened.

And whether it's a sports hero, business mentor, political leader, or any other "model" figure, the process is the same when someone chooses to become a disciple to that person. Authoritarianism, in any form, relies on slow-boil

Same difference when a child learns to walk. They get taught through acceptance—they stumble, get helped up, encouraged, take a few halting steps, smiling and looking for approval, and on getting it, go a few more. Then they reach for more. And they stumble over logs, steps, and obstacles, maybe sit down and cry. And then they get up and go on. They sure don't sit around unhappy for too long, usually no more than it takes to get over a bumped behind.

It takes just a smidgen more than no common sense at all to figure out that
conscious choice, progressive change, and teaching yourself through acceptance instead of judgment makes getting to your goal easier.

Then self-discipline becomes self-discipling—instead of a dirty word, it becomes gradually turning about and redirecting your energy in the direction of your real choice.

I believe there are some rare individuals stricken with the grace to do this, and to them self-discipline has never been a dirty word. For the rest of us out there dealing with budgets, diets, divorces, changes in corporate culture and other severe swerves from our old reality, trying to use self-discipline to adapt has been abysmal.

Make it easier. Clean up your understanding of what is behind self-discipline. Use the process of discipling as a model for "letting you teach yourself" (or "letting yourself learn") how to achieve a goal or adapt to change.

Persevere, remembering that it is always more sensible to use a "Yes" process to pursue a "Yes" goal.

Invisible Dogs On Leashes

I was at one of those gaudy tourist traps on the border between North and South Carolina. Needed to kill a little time traveling. I looked over and saw one of those things that was one the tackiest tourist gizmos ever made. A whole wall of them.

You might remember them. Invisible dogs on leashes: You take a leash, thread some fairly stiff wire down it, and then pull a tail of wire through to the end that attaches to the collar? Then you wire up the collar, so you're walking an invisible dog.

I used to think it was the funniest thing ever. Still do sometimes. Then I got to thinkin about my feelins and how fast they seemed to get so big.

Changed my mind, though, when I realized I was on the end of an invisible leash.

Got to watching and realized a whole slew of us are. Was the tail wagging the dog or the dog wagging the tail? Was the walker maneuvering the leash or vice versa? Look around. Especially just after a cutback has been announced where you work, or when someone is going through divorce or recovering from a death. Just the ordinary stresses and strains of life will do.

How many people do you know or encounter who would say to you, "I just can't help it, I just feel how I feel and there's not a thing I can do about it" or "I just can't seem to change my feelings"?

Now, my uncle Ned, he worked at one of them factories where the line workers did the same ole motions time after time. Schedule was set by the supervisor. Ned never even seen the boss. Everthing was run by the supervisor. Well, you know what, came a day the boss shows up and decides to change ever little thing about how that ole factory was sposed to work. A panic set in is what happened. That supervisor was scared witless that he was agonna lose his job, and my uncle and his pals thunk the same thing.

Supervisor, he started ahuffin' and apuffin' to make sure the boss knew how downright important he was to the operation. As soon as the boss asked him a question about the bobbin winder? It got real clear who actually did the work, and it warnt the supervisor.

Now, imagine that you are like that ole factory and your emotional life is that supervisor. Less'n you exercise your will over 'em, your emotions can act up like that supervisor—they are un-discipled, do whatever is necessary to create the gratification they need, and oh, what havoc they wreak if you decide to begin to make 'em mind!

Your end up on their leash. It's invisible, all right, until that old thing rears up and jerks you around a time or two. And if you decide to get a hold of yourself, watch out. Just like the supervisor is threatened by surprise visits or change in the operation, so your emotions are threatened by your conscious choices to exercise your will differently.

Your emotions require change, just like your body requires food and your mind requires mental activity. They get accustomed to a certain amount of change, and will do whatever it takes to get it. Period. If you have a high need, you may have a more chaotic life, or a more extreme life. Maybe not, maybe so.

Change at the emotional level usually focuses on cause and effect instead of results. Effects are the intermediate reactions to causes, while the result is the last in the series of effects.

Okay, so let's say somebody gives you a hug. Feels good, right? Maybe makes you feel downright contented. Hit's a long lasting thing. That's what most of us would take a holt of. Receiving a hug is the **cause**. Feeling good is the immediate **effect** of the hug. Contentment is (a longer lasting emotion) is hopefully the **result**. Results are long-lasting. They are those states emotionally which most of us would prefer if we knew how to attain and hold them.

You jest think on it, you actually have the power to choose what you feel about 95% of the time. But do you use that power? What would happen, do ya think, if'n you used it more often and in them times chose to put yore aim on results 'stead of effects?

You'da put them emotions on the end of the leash steads lettin' 'em have you on the end of it.

Now, that's a very different thing than suggestin' you deny what you feel or cover it up with a positive quality. It's suggestin' that you begin ta realize you can choose, and the more you use it, the more you find your life agoin' in the directions most folk say they want to see their life goin'.

Duck Poots & Whirlwinds

Back in the country where I grew up we often talked about making mountains out of molehills, but a little further back in the country from where I grew up people talked about events being as important as "a duck poot in a whirlwind."

I reckon we're a lot like other birds too. Like a bunch of hens in the yard. We stir up dust when something thing changes. When we get rattled, we look like a parrot that just hit a ceiling fan. All because of the idea of doing something different. That's where our mule-headedness about - change shows up so clearly: Even the idea of doing something different ruffles our feathers, let alone the demand or requirement.

No matter what you're doing, remember that resistance to change is ultimately about as important as a duck poot in a whirlwind. The tendency to react to every change as if it is overly important—something we can't possibly do because we have always done things another way—is partly based in our belief that we are unrecognized.

If you're not seen or heard, and your success comes in laying low like a duck hunter in the swamp, even if it means no chance of greater success, being called out and told to consider or make a change is painful. It can feel like the possibility is as dangerous as a loose round of birdshot.

Now I know if I tell you (or if you tell someone else) that resistance to change is about as important as a duck poot in a whirlwind, they resist even harder. They will not be told they are unimportant, expendable, or so uninvested in their world they are purely at its whims, gees, and haws.

In addition to food, shelter, and clothing, humanshave four basic universal needs. They are recognition, acceptance, affection, and love.

Most of the time when we make a mountain out of a molehill sized change, or when we run headlong into our resistance about a proposed change, we're running into old unmet needs. Maybe nobody listened, like to that old mockingbird who's claimed the ridgeline of the house his. If he can't allow as how he is the King in 85 different tunes, prancing back and forth on the top peak of the roof, how does he know his offspring are safe to live there? When he hits 90, I know he feels unheard. No challenge has come back. No other mockingbirds have come around, except one, and it just ignored the King. Maybe that's what made him hboller out those five new calls.

People who suffered during changes and whose suffering was not acknowledged, whose ideas and inputs were not welcomed or heeded will resist change. They are in fact, in their resistance, acknowledging their desire for change; they are just doing it backwards. They're running from change like a crawfish facing boiling water.

If you've known all along it could be done more effectively and efficiently and no one ever listened, your resistance is expressing a negative need for recognition and acceptance. And, perhaps, disbelief at how thick your colleagues and bosses might be.

At that moment? Out-crazy the crazies. Give recognition, air and ear space. Just be there and listen, because many times your recognition that their needs have been valid even if they cannot be met dramatically reduces resistance to change. It don't mean they were seen or head or that their needs got met in the past, or even that they may get met now. It means they exist and are heard. Sometimes when you feel like a haint, it's good to be just seen and heard. Makes you real.

Why? I'm thinkin if you know you need to change, admitting it and figuring it out can feel embarrassing. Sometimes everbody goes further, stays longer, and does more than they should. Sometimes everbody comes up short. And the face of a change? Unless you own it, can steer it and make sure it comes out just like you want it to, and everbody else has to do the changing, it's easier.

I think the desire for knowing what to do and doing it well is the biggest satisfaction you can have. "Willing" and "able" are the two siblings of success.

If you're willing and able but nobody will let you or it don't make no never mind that you are, good shame can creep in.

Shame's old dark roots take hold when we decide we're not important. Think about how easy it is for children to decide that their needs aren't important ecause the adults always have their faces in a device. The child who wants to go out and play, that is to have satisfaction in his own work life, to develop mentally, who goes to Dad or Mom and says "Can you play with me?" and Dad or Mom says "Ah, later honey, we will play at 4:00, I've got to be here right now." But when 4:00 comes and they aren't there, the child often can only feel responsible for the adult's choice. They feel badly because they "shouldn't have asked." That's shame. It's created when the world around them tells them they "shouldn't" need time with their adult.

I get real bored with transactional analysis in the workplace. It's still there, though, because we deal with people as parent/adult/child. We can react to one person from any of the three perspectives. Each of us has a predominant role in our relationships; sometimes our role depends on the person with whom we're interacting.

A high level of parent/child-type interactions usually hides an unrecognized sense of shame in the corporate structure. When shame becomes pervasive, factual events take on monumental feeling proportions that ordinarily would be as insignificant as duck poots in a whirlwinds.

The way facts are talked about can help keep them balanced and can help feelings from becoming facts. Let's say you hear someone talk about something and they sound like an old outboard radish—"but-but-but" every other word.

What does that tell you? "But" negates everything said before it. "He is a good employee but . . ." or, "We have a good system but . . ." or, "It's a good car but it needs a new engine."

The only thing "but" does is say that everything you just said before wasn't true. Substitute "and" where you have been using "but," and you acknowledge that the current state needs improvement and that it still has good, valuable and effective components.

The "buts" are a cue that the speaker doesn't feel totally comfortable with what comes after the "but." There may be feelings that they're unaware of or that most likely are shame-based behind the scene. You may never know.

Big things can happen—much bigger than duck poots in whirlwinds. If you keep them in balance by remembering to identify the fact, recognize and respond to the feeling, handle the fact, and hang your thoughts together with "and," you'll keep the "but" out of the air.

Insignificant stuff will stay that way; significant stuff will be manageable.

Ben Franklin And Failure

Ben Franklin: He was a man with a great big mind. In helping frame our early governmental procedures he put common sense adages and logical structures to work in business and government.

That's a lot more than we do most of the time. Most of us don't think—that is, actually engage brain and apply outcome. We do it much less in our lifetime than Franklin did in a year: we have lots of supports that do it for us in our more complex world.

Brains are meant to be more than the guts of a hat rack. They're more sophisticated than computers, faster by far, and better logical structures. They're interactive with the rest of us; I've never seen a hand wave without the stimulus generated by a brain.

Franklin did a good job at thinking and using the product of his thoughts. We'd do better if we followed his habits; at least if we followed his advice.

Fools make folly when they cast reason aside. Reason coupled with imagination creates new ways; reason burdened by dull brains digs ruts deeper.

One of the most useful concepts Franklin developed is a way of evaluating the risks and benefits of reasoning. Anyone in sales and marketing can probably tell you about the Ben Franklin sales closing technique. This old boy I knowed down in Hoehenwald Tennessee lined him up a bunch of women. First by height, and the told all the ones too much taller than he was to step aside. He asked the rest to sort themselves into the ones with career hopes and those happy to lay about the house. Line up the reasons for and against the choice and you see pretty quickly the best way to go.

What happens is that you choose more carefully, looking at the consequences clearly instead of acting on impulse.

When you're going through change, it's even harder to consider the potential outcomes. It's too easy to find yourself in the NO category of life. The first reaction to major change—especially if it hits you in the wallet or in your self image—is almost always NO, I'm not gonna. The second underlying current is a stronger fear of failure instead of hope for success.

Use old Ben Franklin's technique to consider the process of change. You can set up a fairly easy model for looking at the reasons that we are far more attached to failure than to success. Right here's the root the big hog goes for.

If you look at our social expectations, what happens when you have a car wreck? It is, "Oh honey, did you get hurt? Is everything going to be OK? How bad was your car hit?" Or perhaps at a death, the amount of sympathy that is extended. Generally in situations of failure where we all have bad feelings or when most of us have feelings of discomfort, we tend to wallow in a lot of sympathy, comfort, pity and attention. Those are the positive benefits of failure. In work, we see the individual in failure has less required of him or her. Direct relationship.

Now, you might say, "What are the negative benefits of failure?" Obviously, you don't add bricks to a fellow's load if he can't carry a hod—or keep dumping responsibility on someone who demonstrates they can't handle what they've got.

The negative benefits of failure are fairly obvious if you think about how you felt if you have ever been fired. It's a little like being leveled by a steam roller. Money drops, self-respect and self-esteem slink about as low as slug slime. Immunity to viruses and bugs of all sorts decreases. Negative benefits of failure? You bet.

Take a look at the negative benefits of success. You might find it odd to consider the loss of sympathy, pity, comfort and attention as negative benefits of success, but I can reassure you when you begin to move towards the pinnacle of your career that your friends drop off—folks really don't like you too much when you're successful. In fact, you get to be about as popular as pox with your old friends who are still doing what they did.

And if success isn't what you attain, if it's health instead, it's just the same. Ask anyone who has reduced their weight significantly about the number of fat friends who still wanted to be their friend after they got lighter in weight. Face it, few people like you when you succeed at something they'd like to do.

Then if something bad happens it's, "Ah, that's too bad, ain't it a shame, just go get you another one since you've got so much." It's a lonely climb to the top and it's lonely when you get there. It's not necessarily because folks have elbowed somebody off the plateau; it's just plain envy. One of the negative benefits of success is loss of sympathy, pity, comfort and attention.

Conversely, the positive benefits of success are the flip side of the negative benefits of failure. You can see increased self esteem, increased self respect, increased responsibility, increased levels of financial success—the things that go down as negative benefits of failure are the very things that stack up as the positive benefits of success!

How much more familiar are we as human beings with the positive benefits of failure, sympathy, pity, comfort and attention, than with the positive benefits of success—increased self- esteem, increased responsibility, increased self respect, and increased financial rewards?

If you look at the number of twelve-step programs, it's pretty clear we're much more familiar with, addicted to and involved with trying to leave the negative benefits of failure behind.

We don't know a whole lot about living with the positive benefits of success. That's part and parcel of learning to choose—even when it feels awkward. If the payoff for making changes that cause discomfort is isolation and alienation, then what is our mode, what is your motive, what is our drive? What pushes us to go on and go for success?

That's a deep personal choice. You choose for yourself your "driver"—whatever motivates you. For some it's money, things or people. For others, the pleasure of serving or their spiritual values.

Regardless of what drives you, and whether what you're driven to is—sales, marketing, quality improvement, problem solving, or personal transformation, you can't win when you're addicted to the negative benefits of failure.

Take old Ben's way and adopt it. Begin to think about the consequences you get for each set of actions you take.

Look at how the tail is going to wag the dog. And if you don't like it, don't get the dog. Harness up to a new one.

If you use your brain for more than the guts of a hat rack, you can hitch up to the kind of dog whose wag matches the animal you want to see on the front end.

Information Gluts And Future Shock

Have you thought how much more information you get each day as opposed to ten years ago?

Dramatic increases in information generated and promulgated are directly responsible for the increased perception and fact of change.

When oral history was the only form of communication, change occurred much more slowly. It took a long time for conversation in what is now California to get to what is now North Carolina. No optic fibers, telephones, telegraphs, mail carriers—just the months it took to cross the country. No computer modems. No instant transactions. How much more time would it take to change without those tools and without their speedy processing of information?

It's easy to see what's happened if you just do a simple graph of time from 1600 to 1985 and plotting along that line the increase in inventions designed to process information. The curve climbs straight up beginning in the mid-1900s and nearly about falls over on itself.

Consider the increasing speed with which these inventions process information. The primary reason people say change is happening so much faster is, quite simply, the faster you can process information, the faster changes occur.

Business projections that used to take at least a full day to figure now take a matter of minutes using powerful computer programs. We can predict reactions to different market strategies or different occurrences much more rapidly now, requiring us to prepare intervention strategies more quickly.

Some of the ways public events have been handled generate vast amounts of information—all of which are almost accurate, none of which are completely accurate. Each distorts the picture in a different way and creates world-wide ripples at different levels.

Our minds continue to process information at the same rate that they always have, while machines process information more and more quickly. As a result, we lag behind in our ability to create and impact change in our world.

The answer is not necessarily to slow down technology, the answer is to learn how to cope with change more effectively. Once we begin to implement proactive long-term thinking along with an appropriate amount of reactive short-term thinking, we begin to be able to balance this tremendous juggling act a little bit more readily.

If you can't slow down the future, and you can't speed up your mind a lot, you can learn to dance a little better. Dancing a little better means looking at your reactions to change in your life, evaluating how those reactions affect you, looking at additional ways you can think about change, and adding some of them to your life.

That's the skill and art of practicing conscious choice-making. It makes coping with change much easier.

Iron On Iron

Many of us who have been through a lot of change find the experience is like iron chiseling on iron. In becoming who we are, many of the choices we make, their consequences and the experiences we confront are very, very difficult. Oftentimes we're like the new kid who didn't know the winter game of "Crack the Whip" and got on the tail the first time out. We get slung around pretty bad.

Now, everybody has challenging experiences of their own. Common to all is no matter who you are or what the name of your experience is, iron on iron is a tough process. Doesn't matter what it is, "tough" is relative to each of our lives as individuals. Can't compare yours to mine and say mine was harder. Might not of been, to me.

How come I'm so pigheaded? Is it that I get blinders on and just start digging a rut? Only problem there is the shallow difference and the short dimensions between a rut and a grave.

Is it just plain self-centeredness and buried shame? It's like Miss Lucy Ann when she tossed those pretty curls and said, "Why, you know I couldn't possibly need to change—I'm practically perfect in every way!"

I reckon she showed us! The fact that doing something different downright threatens the stuffings out of her is plain as the nose on your face here. She'd a whole lot rather deny she might need to change than face it. You reckon it'll take a telephone pole to land on her to get her to look at it?

When I think about iron on iron, I think about how come it is so hard to make change, what is it that keeps us from being willing to make changes from which we would benefit.

I think we all have flashes of seeing something about ourselves or something about the future that might be coming towards us or some trend that we would really like to be proactive about, you know, the fifth time the same thing happens and you think maybe you should be doing something different.

The way I figure it, needing a telephone pole instead of a toothpick is something related to the experience of being born. If you think about what it is like to be a baby before you're born, it's a pretty good deal. You've got "three hots and a cot"—three meals a day, a place to sleep, no cares or worries except those transmitted through the umbilical cord.

Life is pretty secure and safe. Everything is a big YES. All your needs are met; there's no risk, certainly not such as you might perceive (so far as we know about unborn infants).

But then, no matter when it happens, the big squeeze comes, you get drained, you get pushed out of the birth canal, and unless you have the very fortunate benefit of being born in a warm southern ocean, you emerge into a cold room.

Sooner or later somebody cuts the cord. It is the first experience of separation, of finding yourself separate from your mother, and from then on folks, there is a whole lot of separation. "NO," the keyword of individuation—you, separated from your desire—becomes the most powerful word in your world.

Sometimes iron on iron is the process of seeing ourselves constantly separated from our desires until we change directions. You can watch a pair of unevenly yoked workhorses and see this. The stronger one pulls till the weaker one follows. Sometimes iron on iron is the process that we go through when we change directions and begin to get adjusted to a new one. That would be, yessiree, when you happen to be the one being led.

One of the hardest iron on iron experiences I have ever had was the process of deciding that I really wasn't handicapped. I'd been born with a congenital defect that caused both knees to dislocate. Much of my childhood was spent on the ground as a result, and I grew into my middle school years, in casts, having surgery, trying to get my knees corrected.

I got very comfortable with the concept of being handicapped. I learned there were some real benefits from it, people felt sorry for me, I got a lot of pity and sympathy, and I certainly got a lot of attention from those big red stripes on my legs.

Of course, the trade off was that I couldn't do things that other kids could do. I grew more and more bitter about it. I kept seeing myself as "separate from"—no I can't do that, no I can't run, no I can't swim, no I can't do this, no I can't do that, I'm different, I'm separate.

I became a hard, bitter and self-pitying individual. I don't know what trigger got tripped, or what switch got turned on, but there came a point in time when I decided I really didn't want to see myself as handicapped and in fact, I was about as able as anyone else even though I was different.

If the process of iron on iron meant doing things as outrageous sometimes as hiking on crutches, driving straight-shift Volkswagens with casts on both legs, and ultimately, the challenge of carrying a glass jug down a trail that dropped 300 feet in a quarter-mile, just to see if I could do it, then, by golly, I did it!

It was a process of me being iron, being strong willed (very strong willed) chiseling on iron. I lived in my separateness, not in my ability and what I could do and was, but in what I thought I couldn't do and wasn't.

The chiseling on my character took place in a very difficult and challenging way. There was a lot of re-evaluation of who I was, of what it meant to be me, what I wanted to do, and what I actually could and couldn't do.

A few years after I made that conscious choice I saw someone that I had not seen since childhood, and their first question, to give you a clue where my identity lay, was, "How are your knees?" No more, now.

For people who go after it tooth and toenail, the process of spiritual transformation is also often an iron on iron experience. In the Christian tradition being constantly transformed "from glory to glory" is the process of having the pressure of God impact the willfulness of man.

Many times in business we see a similar process of persons molding into corporate culture, chiseling away at their self identities. At the same time we are chiseling away to learn to fit, we face the pressure of being chiseled on, as well as retaining some of our self as well. Unhappy is the person who becomes their work.

It's easier to let the outside hammer away at us. It's hard to lift and lie down under the hammer at the same time. It's hard to say, "Hammer on! If iron on iron it must be, so be it!" not knowing what the Creator will remake in the created!

Again, though, you can stand it until you die. And the strongest character is that born of iron chiseling away at iron, forging strength with which to face change, strength bound with flexibility and proactivity.

Life's Laws Of Physics: Choice Is All There Is

Sometimes I think it should be "life's slaws of physics." There is a fundamental law of physics that applies to us in life in a lot of different areas, especially as we deal with change. It can sho-bud make you feel like shredded cabbage dress with vinegar and longing for mayonnaise.

It is: For every action there is an equal and opposite reaction. You might call it the pendulum effect.

Because we are so accustomed to NO driving our lives, we find any time we start looking at YES, we tend to go hog wild. You can see this in divorce. Many folks recently divorced (the marriage was the NO) go off the Richter Scale in terms of social life and dating and acting like adolescents (the perceived YES when they were in the NO).

Sometimes the calmest people go wild with grief. Sometimes a person who acquires sudden wealth spends out of control. When you see somebody bouncing off the walls, that's when you're dealing with "life's slaws" or "life's laws of physics."

In fact, you can take a look at how you divide the world into opposites and much more clearly see life's laws of physics and how they apply to change. Consider the things we devalue. I mean, nobody likes being fat, ugly, old, poor or sick. We value very highly in the positive being healthy, well, rich, young, attractive.

Yet, most of us are—or would like to be—in the balance. We're pretty much right where we happen to be because of timing, choices we have made or the genetics we have been dealt. It's the only place we can be.

We can gradually move some of those opposites into more balance—for instance, if I'm ugly, I can always have cosmetic surgery or I can use make-up or I can wear a paper bag or I can change the way I think about myself.

There are some pieces in life with which we are stuck. They relate to how we deal with life's laws of physics.

What are you going to do? Are you going to bounce off the walls, or are you going to settle down in the middle and learn how to live out of choice as much as you possibly can?

Choice is, after all, the best option. Aging, taxes, and, to some extent health, are topics you pretty much are stuck with. You will age, pay taxes, and probably get sick sometime. It's a sure thing you'll die. Weight and attractiveness you have more control over.

Attitude and balance—there you have almost complete choice. Think about it: Excessive choices in one direction lead to extremes. Balanced choices let you take charge of your life in spite of events around you. You can choose your attitude about it at every moment, so long as you're willing.

When you bounce off the walls just because you're used to it, you're part of life's slaw: A mish-mash of shredded cabbage flung about the kitchen with a mad dash of carrots and some sort of moistener. I use mayo and vinegar for a good bite. It's still slaw: Not very distinguishable taste, often lukewarm in cafes, and really rotty when it's stale. Consistency and slaw are mutually exclusive, in cooking and in life.

On the other hand, monitoring and choosing about your actions puts you one up on life's laws of physics. If you minimize the swing on some or all of your actions in certain dimensions, you create less backlash.

More room to get what you want to do done.

Better opportunities to move forward instead of staying in perpetual cleanup.

Green And Slimy Lazarites

A friend of mine used to say I'd been through more change than anyone except a post-surgical transsexual opting for sex change reversal. The number of times I've reinvented myself, shifted to another way of being, turned around and tapped my heels three times and more is just dadgum innumerable.

The number of times any human being bangs on the inside of his or her own tomb, pounding away at the stone, waiting for it to roll away is almost innumerable.

Just as butterflies don't like cocoons, we really don't like being buried alive. We don't like finding ourselves inside the tomb prematurely, and I doubt many of us even like getting to it on time.

If you think about the story of Lazarus, who died, was embalmed, wound, wrapped, buried, rotted, and then, of all things, raised back to life, it becomes a little easier to understand how profound change can be. Ever wonder what state of consciousness Lazarus had in that condition and what he might have been thinking as he came to?

Think of the times that you've found yourself in an enigmatic situation in your career or your personal life and have been unable to see an out. By sitting there and looking for windows where once you could see no doors, you are able to see the gravestone rolling away.

Often, as I've said, if the Big Boss can't get my attention with a toothpick, He uses a telephone pole.

A lot of times when it comes to that point of resurrection, the divorcing from the old life and the embarking into the new life, we desire a toothpick and we require a telephone pole.

And so it is when we are making changes.

I would rather have the toothpick to help me remember I need to hear more effectively and I know I really need a telephone pole. I keep thinking things can be like they always have been and I can still end up somewhere different.

Let's say you're working in an environment where your business has just been buried by change and you feel like you are in a grave. Literally, maybe you don't know where your future is headed. Maybe your company has gone down the tubes. Or you're at a dead end because you don't know what to do and the economy is in such a situation you're not sure you can find a job.

Remember the symbolic nature of life. You are literally like Lazarus. You're bound up in the grave cloths of the old, waiting, just waiting for the stone to be rolled away. Well, symbolic death—no matter how easy or how beneficial it is in the long run—is simply no fun.

The feelings you have when you find yourself bound up in the grave cloths are the same feelings you have the first day you sit down at a computer, the first day you learn a diagnosis isn't deadly, that you passed a dreaded exam, the moment you "got it" about a particular process. You feel fear, anxiety, ultimate irritation, annoyance, feeling rather awkward because you don't know what to do.

We are a lot more equipped to be resurrected than we are to go through the dying process. Even though death is more difficult and resurrection is a relief, death precedes resurrection.

Can't have resurrection without death.

Those little brown woolly worms that predict and then hole up for the winter become ice balls when the weather gets cold, and thaw out in the spring to become beautiful moths? I doubt they're too wild about being frozen into a chunk of ice, but it comes with the territory.

So when you find yourself feeling the feeling that comes with change in a business or personal environment, yes, by all means grieve whatever you feel like you're losing. Also be a green and slimy Lazarite, someone who is already raised from the dead on the inside, looking for life, watching for and letting the door be rolled away so you can get about the business of living in the next level.

We each will probably change careers three or more times. Our businesses will be dramatically changed through international events, cash flow crisis, start-up operations, sales and merger diversities—and the ability to continue to resurrect will be critical in the '90s and the 21st century.

Out Of Fear And Into Longing

Each time I look at situations where change has occurred with a minimum of stops and starts, I find one consistent factor: The folks involved have moved from motivation due to fear to motivation generated by longing.

It sure is easy to see the reason. What happens when you're afraid? Your frame of reference, the factors that cause you to have the picture of the world that you have, gets very narrow.

Usually it focuses on whatever is necessary to insure your own survival.

Competition becomes a hallmark along with other indicators of a traditional environment threatened by change. Cooperation goes out the window.

People who might have once explored become fearful. Folks of high ethical standards become moralistic. The delight in the useful is replaced by a drive to maintain status quo.

Instruction replaces the experimental, the mentoring that comes with cultures passing on their healthy uniqueness.

You can lead an obedient horse to water, and it won't drink unless it's thirsty. Get thirsty. Long for excellence. Develop a passion for living, thinking, making choices. Get committed to choosing.

That will help you move from action driven by fear to action emerging from longing.

Motivation By Provocation

Friend of mine, Mookie, she said —you shouldn't oughta ever tell certain somebodies they couldn't do something.

Mookie was right. Doesn't matter that she was a wrinkled albino prune, older than God, deefer than a post, and plain old simple (not like "simple-minded", just unsophisticated simple). She made strict Quakers look extravagant.

Remember how it is that most of us rebel when we get told we shouldn't do something? Well, that's motivation by provocation.

I don't know if you read the story about Granpaw's Black Hat yet. It's a classic example. What it doesn't say is that his wife, Sullie, had just told him he had better not go out there to mow the yard because it was fixin' to come down a big rain. So of course, being provoked, Grandpaw suited up and went to mow in the middle of a flood. That's how come they could see him from higher up on the ridge.

Some people can be motivated by provocation into doing some pretty phenomenal things—exceeding previous performance, performing unthinkably hard feats, doing what everyone says is impossible to do. Sullie—she's smart—pointed out that if you tell someody they can't and watch them do it. She says that's how we got to the moon, transplanted hearts, created freeze-dried foods, invented those little sticky notes and who knows what else.

When you're the person who's supposed to initiate change, you might want to take a look at who can be motivated by provocation. A person who just up and agrees instead of rebelling is a good candidate for other types of motivation. They need a different variety of carrot in front of their nose.

When you're leading an organization through change, look at all the people. Look at who buckles and who thrives on pressure. Create what needs to be created for each person or group of people according to what motivates each person or group.

The Myth of Security

"Don't you believe it, it's a lie, sure as you're reading this. Ain't no such thing as security. Nor safety neither," Delores shook her head. "You just think about it.

"Remember how it was before divestiture in the phone companies waaay back when? Only had one—maybe two—Ma-Bell and AT&T? Remember how everybody thought if you worked for the phone company you had a job for life?

"Ain't no such thing as security in a job or anywhere else. Everything short of God Almighty, in my experience, will change. Risks of all manner will still exist." She'd put down her pencil and had her head resting on her knuckles.

Divestiture, court-ordered, changed the phone company forever. Nobody who works for the phone company knows where they're going to be for long, seems like. Now? Land lines are all but extinct, there are forty-leven cellular carriers, and about eighty percent of people over 60 have smart phones.

Customers sure don't know about how to use the system—alternate services, whether to rent or buy the telephone, whether to get an Android or an iPhone, how mych memory to get. service and repair plans. Remember when phone bills were just one page? That's long gone!

Imagine how it would be to work in the pre-divestiture days, when only Ma Bell and AT&T duked it out!! You might have thought you'd have a job for years and then all of a sudden didn't have any idea at all where you'd be. Or where you might have to go to keep on working, under what conditions. Whew!

Ain't no such thing as security. Who promised it to you anyway? Where is it written that you had a right to a job with the same company, persistently climbing the ladder of success and promotions over the years?

Where is it written that life is even fair? Let alone work or career? Or that it would go your way all the time? If you think that, your level of erroneous belief is really high.

There is no such thing as security, fair is what you take your pigs pickels and pies to, and life does not always go the way you want it to. You can be driving down the road and have some fool run into your car and kill you. You can be working along and have your company get sold out from under you by the boss in East Egypt—without your even knowing it. You can expect roast beef for dinner and get hot dogs.

Give it up! Realize that security in anything is a myth. Only that which is unchangeable is secure. Whatever it is that you can determine and know 100% as unchangeable is worth deeming secure.

So how do you work with the rest of life? Maybe you decide nothing is secure and you're not going to put your need for security in anything.

How do you cope with change if nothing is secure? Those folks who worked for the phone company when it broke up? All they had were choices.

Choices are the only option you will have until you die.

Don't tell me, "I don't have a choice." You do. You always have a choice, certainly about how you feel. You may be unable to alter an event of change in your life, such as job loss, illness, or disaster. You still have the power to choose how you feel.

Fact is, your ability to choose is guaranteed you as long as you're not in a deep coma or altogether dead. That's security.

Rolling Uphill

So you've realized you can't stay in a cave, you're going to be afraid when you're going through change, it's ok to change careers, to monitor how you use your ability to create rebellion inside yourself, and that in fact you can stand change until you die.

You've gotten on the stick and taken a look at how you beat yourself into failure using self-discipline instead of leading yourself to success. Hopefully, you've started leash training your emotions, taken a look at the real significance of the changes you face (usually about like duck flatulence in a tornado). You've realized that no matter how hard it is, you're willing to risk getting attached to the positive benefits of success in change through choice. This is what choosing to roll uphill in the face of change looks like.

Change is happening so much faster these days! Why? Because of the speed with which information can be accessed and processed. It's clear that change can happen a whole lot faster than we can create and adjust to it.

True too, that personal change is like being hammered flat on an anvil. Bouncing off the walls is little help except to keep you dizzy and still unadjusted.

Yep, you'll resurrect sometime. Maybe if you want to you can move from being motivated by fear to being driven by a longing. Maybe you can get motivated without having to have it come through provocation.

Maybe you realize your security lies in your ability to commit to what is unchangeable and to remember choice is where your power is.

If you do, you're ready to look at the fact that when you make a change, whether you decide it needs to happen, make it happen, or are the one to whom it happens, you'll learn to roll uphill to make it stick.

You know how change goes. Somebody says do it, somebody starts it, the people affected by it grumble along and here in a little while, everybody quits trying.

Changes become long-lasting when folks persist in rolling uphill against the old familiar patterns, for about twice as long as it feels good.

Doubt it? Look at corporate culture change, diet, savings or exercise plans. In implementation they often fall short. Maybe you work in an exceptional place where it's different. Great. Then remember how hard it was to roll uphill long enough to make the change a lasting one, and help others remember by being a model when change is required again in the future.

It's a place where you can exercise choice. Rolling uphill exercises your will in the most powerful way: you're deliberately choosing how you think, feel, and act in the service of something you want, in response to change you're facing.

That's personal power. That's why choice is the power in the face of change.

The Rut and the Grave

I am indeed a creature of habit. Who's not? I have my ways, and I like them. And if I didn't, I'd certainly change them. At least that's what I say. The truth is, I am as happy as a clam in my ways.

You know what I mean: think about it. You have a television show you like. Maybe it's a crime, or a drama, or the Sunday afternoon soccer—or football, depending on your culture—game.

Every time your show comes on, there you are. Ten minutes before, you were heading to the refrigerator, tossing a bag of popcorn in the microwave, dreaming and longing for that nice soft recliner with the easy-up footrest. That was last year.

This year, you just parked a micro-fridge fridge on one side and a three-shelf table with a little microwave on the other. Turned to open so you don't have to get up. Three boxes of popcorn and a shaker of something (not salt!) on the bottom shelf, and the television guides on the middle. Along with the remote, parked right there at command central.

In the fridge you have all the cold ones—lite or diet—closest to you and the full-on beer and soda farthest. Oh, yes—how about a couple of candy bars and some string cheese in the door? That's more like it. Your version of "manworld"—even if you're a woman—right there. Your version. Patterned on the groove you wore, the habit you developed.

I'm pretty happy in mine: Get up, put on my "fur" as I tell the cat, and head for kitchen. Assess: Is there wet food in the refrigerator or do I need to pick up a pouch? In the fridge. Pick up his bowl, left hand. Pick up dry food, right hand. And the fact is that I may have wallowed myself a rut.

What makes ruts? Going in the same place over and over again. Most of us have ruts: repetitive ways of performing tasks, going places, sayings, thought processes, emotional patterns. Funny, though. If you do what you've always done, chances are, you'll get what you've always gotten. Now, that's a rut!

And the only difference between the rut and the grave is the depth and where the ends are.

Seasons of Change Paradigms

Small comfort, this. Some comfort when you remember how cyclical life is. We go from spring to summer, fall and winter—from birth through youth to maturity and old age. Businesses go from start-up to development, fruition, and—sometime, somehow—closure.

So it is with all change. Change occurs when the party who has the authority to initiate it deems change necessary, and when the party undergoing change participates.

There are different types of change. A good many occur as result of time and **development**: most babies follow a very similar sequence of when they develop different abilities. My cousins Lizzie, Maggie, Toadey and Poley all learned to crawl at 11 months and walked by 13 months. Poley he could toddler-run by 15 months, but Maggie took til she was 18 months. Toadey skipped walkin altogether.

Developmental changes occur as a natural process of the cycle of life. They occur in the growth of a seed to a plant and then to reseedin' and in the birth and life cycle of a business or relationship.

Such changes are reasonably predictable at the big level. They cause discomfort, occur at usually predictable points in time and have typically known consequences. They cause temporary upheaval. When such changes occur in situations involving a number of people, such as in a company or family, predictable consequences become less predictable. Personal, less visible issues increase in number.

Another type of change, one that often emerges in developmental changes that involve a number of people, is more **transitional**. If your company is at a developmental change point, it may trigger transitional change as employees relocate, change jobs or careers, perhaps divorce.

When you're in transitional change, life is much less certain than in developmental change. Transitional change is less predictable; it often lasts longer, and its focus on form over function can impede the progress required to keep functional matters going. Still, it has guideposts and markers along the way, and the chaos is knowable. Others have gone where you are going. Oh—and developmental change is still occurring.

Not so in change that is born of and brings transformation.

Transformational change may involve both developmental and transitional change, and it is unlike either. It is the change of chaos, of discovery, of going where no one has ever been before. Or, perhaps, where you have never been before. It's the first trip to outer space, the first heart transplant, the first business of a kind—innovation in expression. Terribly frightening and also exhilarating, it is ungrounded. There are vague, perhaps recognizable markers along the way—since this is a new path, untrodden, there are no sure guideposts.

Individuals may undergo **transformational** change at the personal level in some circumstances. In the transformational process of spiritual development, each person becomes someone different from the next person aspiring to the same goal. Think about the people who worked in the long-gone Saturn division of General Motors. The start up used different rules, different processes, and required different ways of thinking. The people who came were carefully vetted to be open to creative problem-solving, willing to work collaboratively, and were required to complete 200 hours of training a year including systems, technical and soft skills.

They came perhaps not quite convinced of the way things had always been done in the GM-UAW environment, and not knowing that the Saturn venture would be like. Some spent up to a decade being transformed by a culture based on remarkable values that people worked to live out every day, self-directed unstructured work teams, an organization with only five levels between the CEO and the bottom of the org chart, and a commitment to a different kind of car for a different kind of customer. Yes, the business venture didn't make it. I assure you the people who were part of it were transformed.

Business transformation has both the known and unknowable. If you work for a firm pursuing a style of operation previously untried (so far as you know, according to literature and data base searches) then of course there is anxiety. No rules, guidelines, historic antecedents.

Measurements based on best guesses, tentative benchmarks.

How will anyone know if they hit the mark? Perhaps your culture is changing, and your firm is endeavoring to form a new one. That is transformational, and also developmental. Your corporate culture will follow a reasonably predictable developmental process known to those in organization development (or even social work's group process). How it is transformed, however, will be unique to your group and will contain elements of risk localized to choices the change initiators, agents, and targets choose.

The roles we each have in change paradigms vary, as well. The one who decides the change needs to occur and has the power to implement it is clearly the one who initiates it, or the **owner** or **initiator**. They may or may not also be the one who acts it out and implements it in the environment—the **agent** of the change. Needless to say, if you're on the receiving end of the change, you're the person with the bull's-eye pinned on you: the **target**. A sports analogy might be to call the one who calls the shots the coach, the one who delivers them the pitcher, and the one who gets them and is supposed to do something with them, the batter or the catcher.

If you're in the middle of change, it's hard to keep them clear and respond to each need as it emerges in an appropriate manner. It takes considering the highest powered easiest skills and choosing whether to practice them when it's easy and when it's tough.

Thermostats and temperaments

Jim, he leaned over and said real quiet like, "Yore mama hit the change yet?"

"Which one?" I asked him.

"You know—middle pause. Whur she's crazy as an outhouse rat bouncing off the walls with her feelins and wants to keep it could enough to hang meat because of those dadgum hot flashes. She keeps it like a pneumonia hole in the bedroom. I have to come outside to get my acorns to come down off my earlobes I git so cold."

"I can't say as she has," I said, "But I shore have. I'll tell you what, bud, them thar hot flashes make spontaneous combustion take on a whole new perspective.

"I swan, when one hits I can feel the flames starting. I'm hot all over. I seat in places I didn't know I could, like my elbows and the soles of my feet. And I caint think, neither. My earlobes and face turn tomato red.

"I had to reassure a group of people I was helpin learn customer service that I wouldn't explode even though I was bright glowing red."

He laughed. "That sounds about right. Hot to cold in a split second. Sad to mad in less. Glad to giddy in two. She aint right."

"Well what about menopause?" I said. "Men go through hormone shifts as they age too. We're not the only ones afflicted!"

"Naw, little sister, not quite," he said. "We slow down, lose power, and need shoe horns and duck tape because ever bit of testosterone we got has left the building. But we don't git crazy like that and we don't sut the heat off in winter time."

"Just be glad it has a switch," I said. "Open winders in February are not the best option."

Feline anxiety

"Dey, God. I caint git rid of the shakes. Ever since that painter come up in the back yard and stared at me I feel like a marked man." Junior had never seed such a cat before. Hit was dark and sleek with big glowing yaller eyes. He didn't know such a thing existed.

Now, yes, he'd heard what sounded like a woman a-screamin' in the woods a couple of nights and his daddy had told him to stay put and not leave the house. He hung in there, nailing his curiosity to the floor as best he could.

And on that third night, he could't hold back no more and he stepped out on the porch. The light come on, and there hit was. A painter, a catamount. The tawny ghost of the hills. Hit could make a man come running because it sounded like a woman in trouble. Hit'd be the last thing he ever did, though.

Junior, he was lucky. He stood stock still and so did the cat. Hit sot down on its haunches and looked at him, clearly confident and unafraid. Hit knowed it owned the situation. Hit could leap, run, jump, claw and yes out-stare anything.

Junior, he broke out in a sweat and backed up easy like to the door, slipped back in and shut the door real quiet. "I know who owns the night," he said, "and it aint me."

Ever since then, Junior's been as nervous as a long tailed cat in a room full of rocking chairs. Any little sound makes him jump. And if he hears that catamount wailing, he shakes with fear like a possum passing peach pits.

    I don't know if he'll ever git over it, but he needs to, because there's a right smart number of things to do around the place when dark comes. The night aint near as skeert of the painter as Junior is of the night.

Worth Something

"Oh my God," Rufus moaned. "You brung him to work? Why he's so dumb he fell in a bucket of titties and came up sucking his own thumb!"

"Well, what could I do? His daddy said he needed to work, and I had work I thought he could do, and here he is." Jim Bob shrugged.

"That boy is dumber than door nails." Jed chimed in.

It wadn't like Jim Bob didn't know this, and it wadn't like he could do anything about it. When Mamie said, "He's your'n" earlier that morning, he knew what it meant.

Git the boy up, dressed, fed and out the door before she threw a major hissy fit. Why she could sail a dish across the room like a Frisbee® and hit a body with it as easy as anything.

Lester, he couldn't keep a job, if he got up long enough to git one. He couldn't even be counted on to do chores, because he done 'em so porely wouldn't nobody ask him to. In spite of all them years o'larnin, his vocabulary was little more than grunts and waves of his grubby hand. Readin' was strickly off the table. He was best—when you could git him to do anything—doin' simple manual labor. He was like a human tow mnotor when it come to moving boxes and pallets.

"Jim Bob," Rufus sighed, "you know you're some count on a how you got in here and built this place up.

Lester? He aint no count, caint be anything but. Don't go letting him tarnish yer spoon."

"Rufe," Jim Bob said, shaking his head, "they's got to be a place in this world whur Lester fits. Ever peg has its hole. We just got to find it."

Gittin older

I woke this morning thinkin, "Oh mercy, how am I gonna git out of this hyar bed... my back's done gone out." It hurt like forty, makin me almost throw up or want to pass out.

I had to do the things a body needs to do after being in bed all night, and ended up having to push off on my thighs and up at the same time. I remembered something my sister said to me. "We're all pushin' mid70s and our brains feel like we're forty. The problem would be that ever injury we ever had is starting to come back with a vengeance."

"Is that why my body feels like I'm four hundred years old buy my mind still thinks like I'm in my prime?" I asked her.

Myrtle was sittin next to my sister. "Yeah," Myrtle laughed, you're a combo of rode hard and put up wet and long in the tooth. You done worked too hard all yore life and yore gittin old."

"Got room to talk! Yore daddy's so long in the tooth he could eat apples through a chain linked fence and you aint far behind!" I snorted back at her.

"Hope you live long enough for your'n to get that long!" She tossed her head to one side, making the definitive comeback, both a veiled threat and an acknowledgement of reality. I'd hurt myself enough doing stupid and smart things, and sure enough, the old injuries are coming back to haunt me. Who knows how long I might have.

    Every time I think about something being old, the image of a old mule grinning to show itslong, long brown streaked teeth pops up.

Purty and Pretty

"You member Joey? Great Uncle Ludie's middle young'un?" Robie asked. "The one that was born at the top of the ugly tree and hit every branch on the way down?" Robie was sitting on the porch in his overalls, rared back in a split cane bottom chair. He was a' gazin out longways at the pasture and 'mirating over his farm, nestled in a valley between two tall mountains.

"Ayuhh," his wife, Ootie, responded. "he was, the last time I seed him, more than a little on the rough side of purty." She was peelin and cuttin apples to strang and dry. She leant over to look twargs the back to make sure the dadgum hound wudn't eatin em after she strung each slice on the cotton twine.

"Funny how that happens. His daddy wuz a looker, but his momma looked like a 18-wheeler rearranged her face. Twarnt nothin symmetrical-like. His older brother and younger sister look like Ken and Barbie dolls." Robie scrotched his chin and looked up, like the wuz callin up memories of how Joey's momma and daddy looked. Then, of the whole family with Joey in the middle of the three children.

"Well, you never know. But he shore resembles his momma more than his daddy," Otie pronounced. "Pore thing. He'll find the piece that fits his puzzle."

A Pointless Job

I don't know about you, but I've done jobs that were as simple and repetitive as passing a pack of white spongy snack cakes from one hand to the other. The person next to me could have just as easily gotten it out of the box themselves.

Yes, there are a lot of jobs that are as pointless as nailing Jell-O to a tree in the grand scheme of things. But we do seem capable of making the simplest things more complex, or breaking them into little teeny weeny parts.

While breaking jobs into sets of steps or actions might make it easier in the moment to see where a change might be good, or if you can always keep the bigger picture in mind, but.... that doesn't mean the job adds value to the customer. That extra motion in no way enhances the product, makes it more valuable to the customer, or decreases the cost of production.

And doesn't mean the person standing there passing the widget from left to right has any idea why they do what they do except someone pays them to stand there and do it. Why not just combine the two stations so the next person can get the item with their left hand and install it with their right?

Oh wait. That might imply nailing Jello to a tree works.

See , if yore thinkin this is how processes get improved, the chances are that you're scratching where it ain't itchy. And that doesn't make it better.

Getting' Close to Finishing

My sister is an expert knitter. She could raise up and throw out a sweater about every week if she cared to. She cats on and off, loops the loop, circles around, stabs it, spears it and does whatever else she does to make a row of stitches.

I just try to stay out of the way. She pretty much does the same when I'm gardening. But we have something in common. We both say, "We're getting down to short rows" when we get close to the end.

I wondered why that was, and it does come from farming. In every field, there's unlikely to be rows of an even length unless field is absolutely a rectangle. On the narrower part? Usually where you finish up? The rows will be shorter.

What does that have to do with anything? If it's the end of something, how likely is your attention to be as fresh as it was, as good as it has been, and do you have what you need to finish it?

Or is it just a self-reassuring phrase that the end is in sight?

The Blight of Terror

I have a fury that is red-eyed, forked-tailed, and can be downright mean that is really a tiny terrified small creature. That tiny terrified creature hiding behind the flaming dragon mask is just trying to protect itself from whatever real or exaggerated threat it sees.

Sadly, it's had somebody point a flamethrower in its direction one time too many and now even the unannounced lighting of a match can make it fire up and throw off thunder and lightning to back the heat up.

But it's still a shadow show, a light throwing the shadow of a small frightened kitten in such a way that looks it looks like an enraged panther, huge, big tailed, yaller eyes spittin sparks, long claws up on tippy toes.

The amount of adrenalin that show generates is huge. It leaves me shaking worse than a possum trying to pass a peach pit and feeling as redfaced as a crawfish in boiling water. It's good for a prime shame attack.

Now I make up that men wouldn't be bothered a bit by the trash this can create. I make up that they'd shake off the butt-hurt and go right on as if nothing happened. I'm note sure I know how to hold that space it but I know it's important ot learn to do. To not internalize the pain and anguish of reacting to something with a 16" gun when a BB gun would be more than adequate.

You can mow down a whole row of people who once loved you when you git hit by the blight of terror. And they may or may not stand back up in the face of it.

Not Up to Snuff

Jimmy looked up from his book. "You look like you was sent for but couldn't come," he said. He was writing something, like he allus did, in that little black book he tied up with strang.

"Well, I was feeling off," I said.

"Yeah, I've seen ye look better. Kind peaked, eh?" Jimmy looked over his half glasses.

"Ayuh. Down in my back. I've felt like the off-scourings of black despair for a few days with it." I nodded agreement. "What are ye a writin?"

"Oh, just a few notes."

"I see."

"Shore hope you git to feelin better."

"I thank ye; next time I'll try to look I came when I was called for."

That dog won't hunt.

"Now, look, Lonnie," Demp said, "I know you want to do this and badly. But you got to understand: that dog won't hunt."

"Why, Demp," Lonnie said, "you've saif that about ever ideer I had about this. I know yore agin women doing physical labor, but we need the help and they;'re willing to work. I don't git it."

"Well, for one thing, about the time them women got out yonder in the fields, all their husbands would come a running to beat us to a pulp." Lonnie was emphatic.

"Not if they're all gone to find work somewhere's else! Dagnabbit, Lonnie, that's why we need the women's help. It's got nary a thing to do with their invisible by God men who aint hyar!" Demp got up and slammed his chair down.

"I reckon I see yore point, Demp," Lonnie said. " you don't need to get all het up. Just the thought of that Hoffstetler boy coming after me though—he's built like a bull!"

"How are we gonna handle this? You say they aint no way to git them women to work without offending their husbands, most of whom would just as soon kill us as look at us. I'm worried we aint going ter git the crops in. Aint neither one of them dogs'll hunt."

Suzy come out of the house dryin her hands on her apron. "Why don't you take a trip to town where all the men went and ask them? In the time you done spent jaw-jacking about it you coulda come and gone twice."

"Why Suzy, I didn't mean for you to hear us!" Lonnie hung his head sheepishly.

"Well," she said, "you are sitting underneath the open kitchen winder. I don't about their wives, but if you didn't support me, I wouldn't do it. And I bet none of them boys wants their crops to rot in the field, and would be proud for their families to help out." She eased back inside.

"Demp, that idea is a dog that'll hunt, you reckon?" Lonnie sighed.

"Ayuhhh." Demp agreed.

Cheapster | Like a Hair in a Biscuit

Maurice was talkin to Doris, tellin her about a man at work he reported to.

He said, "You remember Bob, don't you? That old boy from up in the country who was so cheap he could dig the grand canyon looking fer a nickel?"

"Yeah," Clara said. "I do. He reused ever paper sack we had so many times I though he was gonna name each one.

"Well," Maurice said, "We've got a new one. We caint git no supplies nor nothin we need. Use it up, wear it out, make it do is his motto. That dadgum Theo is so tight, he climbs out the window so he doesn't wear out the door hinges."

"Oh mercy," she responded, "we had one like that—Mabel was her name. If she thought something was missing why she'd hang on to it like a hair in a biscuit. She'd spend seventy-five dollars looking for a one dollar pen."

Grinning like a possum eating saw briars

Ollie shook her head back and forth. "If you've ever tangled with a saw briar, you'll know it. Now yore people might call it a cat briar, but you'll definitely know it. Hit's tough, viny, and the briars stay put and just drag through your skin like saws. Deer love to eat it's bulb root, a purty pale layered thing that kind of reminds me of a water lily all closed up. You can almost see through the petals.

"Moonshiners loved to have it growing around their still cause them damn lowland revenuers wouldn't even try to git through it. Them and laurel hells. That's what we called them thickets of mountain laurel and rhodydendrum that was sp close a child couldn' crawl through 'em." She looked off a far piece. "Neither would the law."

"How do the deer eat the root bulb if it's so tough and spiny?" I asked.

"Oh Lordy, the deer take after the possum on this one," she said, laughing. "Possums can get around the brars and snip em off. They grin the whole time they're a-eating them thangs. Like this."

And she broke into a toothless wide grin and laughed. "Grinning like a possum eatin' saw briars! Aint that sumpthin? They look like they're lovin ever minute of it!"

Confused as a termite in a yo-yo.

"Now, I don't mean to slight ya, Sam, but yore not quite right right now." I said it as kindly as I could. I could ell I was shuffling from one foot to the next.

"What on earth do ya mean?" He said. "I'm as right as rain."

Well, I thought to myself. That'd be a lot better than whur we're at now. I come to take him to the doctor, only he says it's next week and not this and the doc says this week. Right now we're about as right as heavy fog rolling in with low to no visibility.

"Well??" He said. Sam looked a little stern, like he wadnt gonna take no guff from anybody. "Jes' how am I not quite right?"

"To start with," I said, taking a deep breath. "today's Tuesday, not Monday."

"Ay-uhh," he nodded.

"And I'm not here to carry ye to tha grocery store." I went on.

"How'm I sposed to eat?" He asked.

"That's another topic,: I said.

"So?" He said.

"We're a-goin to the doctor today. The grocery store run is tomorrow." I tried to say it matter of fact, like saying 'a chair has four laigs.'

"No, hit's next week I'm a-goin to the doctor's. I know it is,: he said. "You caint fool me."

"What would it take for you to know it's this week instead? Do we need to call up Doc Moss and see if his nurse can pull up the schedule? If she says it's so, would it be so?" I asked.

"Hit would," he said, lifting his chin with a tad of pride.

Well, of course, it was this week and she said so and they talked a minute.

"You know," he said, "I was a confused as termites in a yo-yo."

(Yo-yo's were originally made of wood.).

Need a little help? We'd be glad to see if there's a fit.

When you're looking for coaching, learning, speaker services or planning support for changes, or for building sturdier workforces, we can help.

Reach out! We'll at least visit and have a good time.

epower@elizabeth power
|
epower@epowerandassociates.com

www.ingramcontent.com/pod-product-compliance
Lightning Source LLC
LaVergne TN
LVHW011425080426
835512LV00005B/269